CONFESSIONS
of a Beginning Theologian

Elouise Renich
Fraser

InterVarsity Press
Downers Grove, Illinois

InterVarsity Press
P.O. Box 1400, Downers Grove, IL 60515
World Wide Web: www.ivpress.com
E-mail: mail@ivpress.com

©*1998 by Elouise Renich Fraser*

InterVarsity Press® is the book-publishing division of InterVarsity Christian Fellowship/USA®, a student movement active on campus at hundreds of universities, colleges and schools of nursing in the United States of America, and a member movement of the International Fellowship of Evangelical Students. For information about local and regional activities, write Public Relations Dept., InterVarsity Christian Fellowship/USA, 6400 Schroeder Rd., P.O. Box 7895, Madison, WI 53707-7895.

Cover photograph: Lance Nelson/Stock Market

ISBN 0-8308-1519-8

Printed in the United States of America ♾

Library of Congress Cataloging-in-Publication Data

Fraser, Elouise Renich, 1943-
    Confessions of a beginning theologian / Elouise Renich Fraser.
    p. cm.
    ISBN 0-8308-1519-8 (alk. paper)
    1. Fraser, Elouise Renich, 1943-   . 2. Theologians—United
States—Biography. I. Title.
BX4827.F73A3 1998
230'.044'092—dc21
    [B]
                                                                      97-50067
                                                                         CIP

20	19	18	17	16	15	14	13	12	11	10	9	8	7	6	5	4	3	2	1
15	14	13	12	11	10	09	08	07	06	05	04	03	02	01	00	99	98		

For
Diane Renich Kelley
and
Paul King Jewett,
theologians who tell the truth

Preface

Several years ago I sat on our chapel platform and listened as a colleague introduced himself to a group of seminary friends. I was next on the program. He spoke with ease, confidence and gratitude about the way God had led him since childhood into his current vocation. Though he's several years younger than I, he'd already been places I'd never even thought of visiting when I was his age. I enjoyed hearing his story. I also grew increasingly uneasy about describing my own journey. His life seemed far more adventuresome than mine. Both of us are systematic theologians. But we didn't become theologians in the same way, or according to the same timetable.

This book is about how I became a theologian. I've written it in the form of personal witness, drawing on some of my experiences as a child, student, church member and seminary professor. I always believed my life was rather ordinary: nothing to get excited about, certainly not the stuff of dramatic testimonies. I still don't believe my life has been unusual. Yet I want my students and friends to know some of what happened to me along the way from there to here—where I found God, and how God found me.

But there's more to it than that. I've never understood why everyone doesn't want to be a theologian. After twenty-five years of studying and then teaching theology, I'm still dismayed when Christians are suspicious of theology and theologians. I wince when seminarians and preachers drop antitheology comments or jokes into sermons bursting with theological insight. Sometimes it seems almost obligatory—a rhetorical flourish designed to win a congregation's trust or approval. Whatever the preacher is, she or he isn't one of *them*. We can rest easy because we're all on the same side, glad we're not bogged down in utterly useless debate about things no one cares about anyway.

Hence this small book celebrating theology and theologians, an introduction to the inner life and outer habits of practicing theologians. I hope the book entices you into becoming a theologian and loving it with all your heart. If you're already on your way, I hope it encourages you to persevere no matter how long it takes and no matter how many detours and dead ends you encounter.

In the long run, becoming a theologian is about far more than becoming theologically literate. It's about becoming a Christian and a human being from the inside out.

I didn't know this when I began. I thought the process would be chiefly academic. It would be about reading books, taking exams and writing papers. Along the way I discovered it's about life and death—yours, mine and Jesus Christ's. It's about learning to discern the extraordinary hand of God in the midst of ordinary time filled with people doing ordinary things.

While I was writing this book, ordinary time and life kept going. Relentlessly. Most noteworthy was a phone call from my sister Diane to tell me she'd been diagnosed with amyotrophic lateral sclerosis, also known as Lou Gehrig's disease. I wrote the last four chapters of the book during and around trips to visit Diane and her family. When I began flying to Houston, Diane was still minister of education and administration at a large Southern Baptist church in Pasadena, Texas. Several months later she retired in order to focus physical and emotional energy on her immediate family and on preparing for whatever might come next. Taking pieces of this book, and finally the completed manuscript, with me to Houston became a way of connecting with a sister I'd known until now mostly from a distance. And so I've also been learning to be a sister to Diane, from the inside out. Getting ready for her death, and for mine. Wondering where God's hand might be in all this anguish.

Paul King Jewett, my systematic theology professor at Fuller Seminary, first encouraged me to become a theologian. He did more than just talk with me about it. In his teaching and writing he demonstrated the difference it makes when theologians tell the truth. Not truth in the abstract, but the truth about God's ways with us. Truth understood not simply with our heads or even our hearts, but with our whole lives. Truth that becomes visible when what's happening between us today connects or doesn't connect with what we say we believe. This book is the truth as I've understood it with my life up to now.

As I wrote this book I was conscious of my family in the background, especially my parents and my three sisters. Some would tell things differently, or not at all. I've tried to keep the focus on myself, and on the way that being a member of my particular family of origin both gifted and challenged me as I became a theologian.

I've been cheered and moved along from the start by my daughter Sherry, my son Scott and his wife Megan. Their interest in family history and their parents' lives sometimes surprises and always touches me. Finally, I'm unspeakably grateful for the faithfulness of my husband David, who has witnessed firsthand more of this journey than anyone else.

1

Getting Started

MY HEART POUNDED AS I KNOCKED timidly and stepped through the door to meet my faculty adviser for the first time. I'd been out of college nine years and was nearly thirty years old. My husband and I had just moved to California with our young children, Scott and Sherry. David had been accepted as a student in Fuller Theological Seminary's master of divinity program. To our surprise, Fuller had just announced a 25 percent tuition rate for spouses of full-time students. When David's mother offered to pay my tuition, it seemed there was nothing to prevent me.

My faculty adviser was kind, but I didn't have a clue how to answer his first questions. Why had I enrolled at Fuller? What was my goal in studying theology? All I knew was that I'd always wanted to study theology. Concrete plans for *doing* something with my master's degree were hazy. The thought of teaching theology hadn't even entered my mind.

I hate looking and sounding like a beginner. Making mistakes and asking questions. Not sure yet where I'm going, much less how I'm going to get from here to there. Afraid of what might happen along the way. But God loves beginners.

Becoming a theologian is about becoming a beginner. It isn't about whether you're old enough, young enough, smart enough or good enough. It isn't about going to seminary, becoming a church worker or seeking ordination. It isn't about making an appointment with a career counselor or taking a battery of tests to see whether you're cut out for theological studies. And it isn't about knowing what you'll "do" with theology.

From a different angle, it isn't about becoming someone else, changing your personality or leaving your past behind. And it isn't about becoming dull and dry, giving up fun and excitement, retreating from the world to attain some more exalted existence.

Becoming a theologian is about accepting God's invitation to get started. It's about doing things beginners do. Beginners ask questions even though they're afraid some are dumb questions. They make mistakes even though they want to get things right the first time. They accept help whether they've asked for it or not. They don't try to figure everything out on their own. They have fears, hopes and expectations. They're full of enthusiasm and aren't embarrassed or apologetic when it shows. They make plans and dare to take those first awkward steps.

I was full of fear when I began seminary. Fear of being wrong (I had a need to be right). Fear of doing wrong (I was a married woman with children). Fear of being misunderstood (I didn't want to rock any boats). Fear of being criticized and fear of being ignored. Fear of change. Fear of exposing my limited academic background. Fear of being laughed at, especially behind my back. Fear of not being able to manage everything—children, marriage, finances. Fear of failure.

I felt overwhelmed by how much everyone else knew and how little I seemed to know. Overwhelmed by the immensity of the world of theological discussion and by its strange vocabulary. Overwhelmed by how much reading, listening, thinking and wondering there is to do, and by how little time and energy I had on any given day.

Though I felt like a beginner on the inside, I was afraid to let it show on the outside. I was a woman in a strange land. There weren't many of us women at Fuller that first year. I thought I had to be at least nearly perfect so I wouldn't shame or discredit other women.

My strategy was pretty simple: I just took a deep breath, jumped in and swam for all I was worth. No coaches on the sidelines. No coming up for air to reflect on how I was doing. No admission to myself, much less anyone else, that these were very deep waters that I couldn't negotiate on my own.

I wasn't totally on my own. My husband cared and did what he could to reassure and support me. I also joined a women's group that formed during my first year in seminary. We tried to keep each other sane and in touch with reality, but none of us was experienced in the ways of seminary life. We knew we needed help, so we petitioned the seminary for a woman to counsel us. Sadly, when she arrived the following year I didn't take full advantage of her wisdom. I was still trying to figure things out by myself. If my inner fears became visible to her, they might betray me. Maybe I shouldn't be studying theology.

Back then I believed that if the door to seminary was open to me, all I needed to do was walk through the door. Then it was up to me to work hard at proving it was OK for me to be there. I avoided anything that might cast doubt on my decision to study theology. I rarely asked questions during lectures or class discussions. Instead I sat silently, listening to others ask their questions and make their observations. I was determined not to ask questions that might betray lack of background, inadequate preparation for class or ignorance of some basic theological truth that everyone else in the universe already knew.

Even problems as small as not understanding instructions for an assignment fed my fears. Any sign that I hadn't perfectly understood professors, syllabi, reading and writing assignments or classroom discussion would be enough to unmask me. Everyone would know the truth: I had slipped through the admissions process by accident. I really shouldn't be here.

So I asked almost no questions during classes. And I made no appointments with professors after class unless absolutely necessary. I wasn't one of those seemingly bright and confident students who crowded around the professor after class to talk about the lecture or raise profound issues for further discussion. It was important for me to be mature, responsible, hardworking, disciplined and above all self-reliant. I didn't know how to be a beginner.

Added to this, I wasn't sure how my Bible college background fit into seminary studies. I was grateful for my knowledge of Bible content, but most of the time I didn't want people to know I had a degree from a Bible college that wasn't yet accredited. My training was weak in areas I now realized would have been helpful as background for seminary training. I felt naive, ignorant and uncomfortable conversing about philosophy, literature, drama and art. It seemed too late to become a beginner.

Then there was my family. I had a husband and two young children. When my single friends went out together or talked about things they had done over the weekend, I felt strangely shamed, as though I had done nothing, had no significant conversations, been nowhere important, done nothing to broaden my horizons. I didn't know how to make a bridge between what was going on at home and what was going on with my friends. I also didn't know how to admit there were tensions at home, much less how to deal with them. I believed I had to figure this out by myself as well. Signs of tension at home might prove I was clearly disobeying God's plan for married women with children. There seemed only two options: total perfection or total failure. I didn't know how to be a beginner at home either.

All this was costly. It cost time and energy to maintain my nonbeginner status. By working hard to hide my need for help, I insulated myself from the very people who might have given me wise and empowering counsel. In addition, I perpetuated a false belief that I could protect myself from the evils and unfairnesses of institutional life by turning in a near-perfect performance, by being a good girl.

God invites us to become beginners. To forget about the impression we think we're making. To stop nodding yes when we don't yet understand what the other person is saying. To give up the habit of apologizing for taking up too much time with our questions. To stop trying to do it all by ourselves, not letting anyone know we feel overwhelmed. To stop hiding behind silence.

Beginners don't care what people think of them. They aren't afraid of making mistakes along the way or of having to start over. They don't mind looking and sounding like amateurs. They don't waste time and energy trying to control people's perceptions of them. They're even willing to risk having their efforts wrongly judged as evidence that certain kinds of people are deficient or not suited to the pursuit of theological studies. Beginners just want help. And they want to make progress.

There may have been a golden age when beginning theologians were well versed in Bible content, knew their church's theological and historical heritage and were skilled in reading theological texts. But people like this are the exception at my seminary and in my church. My point is that we have nothing to lose but our false shame when we acknowledge our limitations and set out to get whatever help we need. God invites us to start as beginners instead of pretending we're already half there and need only to fill in a few relatively minor missing pieces.

From the moment we decide to become theologians, God

invites us to be what we are—beginners. The invitation to be a beginner is an invitation to rest. It comes immediately. At the very moment we feel most pressured to look like we know what we're doing, God invites us to rest, to stop wasting our time and energy pretending we're someone we aren't. God doesn't hold the invitation back until we're well along the way toward becoming a theologian or until we've somehow earned the right to a little rest. Nor does God hoard it until we've attained some distant goal. We want to be done with the messiness, awkwardness and embarrassment of starting out. God wants us to rest.

Being a beginner from the inside out means acknowledging that God is in charge of this process. We are not. We can't make ourselves into theologians by sheer grit and determination. We did not and do not create ourselves as persons or as theologians. God does. We can't foresee and plan for all contingencies or rehearse our lines before their time. God invites us to rest from the illusion that we can do this right, that somehow we'll make this endeavor turn out better than past endeavors. Though we bring gifts known and unknown to this process, we have not the vaguest idea how or when God will use them.

Becoming a theologian is like beginning a new relationship. No one has a head start by virtue of past experiences. Each of us must begin on page one. Initially every relationship passes through uncertain waters. So must every theologian—not just once but many times. Being a beginner means standing on level ground with other beginners, giving up the idea that I'm somehow more advanced or more skilled at this business of becoming a theologian. Theologians aren't superwomen or supermen. They're people learning to accept God's invitation to rest.

I know what happens when I lose touch with myself as a beginner. I become anxious and guarded lest I look or sound like a beginner. I lose my ability to wonder, to ask questions, to let my ignorance show and to laugh at myself. I lose my freedom and try to skate without letting go of the rail. I begin second-guessing myself, which leads to failure of nerve and loss of confidence. I become obsessed with what other people think about me and my work. I accept their negative opinions as inerrant. Worst of all, I lose touch with the cutting edge of my life, which is the cutting edge of my theology.

It takes courage to be a beginner. The powers of this world are arrayed against beginners. We feel pressured from within and without to look and act theologically sophisticated. We learn early to cloak ourselves in deceptive armors of competence and self-reliance. They're deceptive because they won't protect us from being hurt and misinterpreted. Instead they place more layers between us and God's surprises. It takes courage to begin laying down the disguises that hide our beginner status.

God loves beginners. In the process of becoming a theologian there are many beginnings. Sometimes we miss the invitation the first time around. But God is patient. The invitation just keeps coming until we're ready to respond. It's never too late. With God, no time is wasted.

2

Ties
That Bind

ELDON AND I DIDN'T PLAY TOGETHER often. He was six; I was only five. Besides, I was a girl. Most of the time he played with his brothers and I played with my sisters.

Eldon's family and mine shared a house. A tree stood in one corner of our back yard. Five or six feet from the ground a board had been nailed between the two main branches of the tree. One day Eldon decided to jump from the board to the ground. He was, of course, superior by virtue of this masculine feat. I followed him and made it up to the board but was afraid to jump. By the time I backed out of the tree, I felt thoroughly humiliated. Eldon had long since run off looking for more exciting things to do.

For several days I returned alone to the tree, hoisted myself up to the board and waited for courage to leap. Each trip down the tree felt like failure. Eldon was right. Girls just weren't as brave as boys.

My secret shame grew until I could no longer take the pressure. Early one evening, just before supper, I approached the tree yet again, firmly resolved not to back down this time. I changed my strategy. Instead of looking down and waiting for courage to leap, I closed my eyes, held my breath and jumped.

My flimsy shoes provided no cushion against the shock of hard ground against my legs. I screamed silently. Then I got up and walked as normally as possible across the yard and into the kitchen, where my mother was preparing supper. In a subdued voice I reported that I had just jumped from the tree.

I didn't tell Eldon about my triumph. He might demand that I prove myself by jumping again. I had no intention of doing it again.

There is a gulf between the world of women and the world of men. I spent years gazing across this gulf to the other side, wanting desperately to make an impression on the world of men. I longed to be acknowledged as a real actor, not dismissed as "just another female." I wanted to be different, the exception to the rule. To this end I've jumped repeatedly, especially while becoming a theologian. I set male theologians up as a standard by which to judge my progress. I wanted to belong to the club.

Gender is a tie that binds. It's a connection I can't run away from, a basic piece of my identity I didn't choose. Clustered around gender are other ties that bind me as a theologian. Becoming a theologian has meant attending to these ties instead of overlooking, minimizing or trying to get around them.

As part of becoming theologians, God invites us to stop running from things we'd rather leave behind. To take a closer look at what we've inherited. To acknowledge where those ties bind both negatively and positively, and to accept this as an ongoing theological task, not just a preliminary move or side interest.

When I began seminary I was already painfully aware of my gender. I could name ways it had made a difference in my upbringing and my church experience. In seminary not every woman in my entering class wanted to be labeled a feminist.

Nonetheless, most of us were aware of our gender and interested in exploring the difference it made in our approaches to ministry. I invested time and energy in this, meeting with a support group of seminary women and participating actively in two Christian feminist organizations committed to seeking justice for women in church and society.

My seminary professors, all white males, passed on valuable tools and skills. Several provided gracious support and encouragement. I began looking into Greek and Hebrew Scripture texts, reading biblical and theological commentaries, comparing Scripture translations. I quickly became disillusioned with so-called scholarly objectivity and increasingly excited about other ways of understanding well-known Bible texts about women. Perhaps there was more good news in the Bible than I had thought, especially for women.

In pursuing this I put myself on the line. This wasn't about abstract ideas; it was about me. It had implications for my marriage and my mothering, and for my development as a theologian. My husband David was cautious. We agreed to embark together on what turned into a six-month exegetical and theological investigation of what the Bible says about women. We also agreed in advance to abide by what we found.

I was uneasy. What if my newfound excitement was misguided? Maybe all those men and women who taught about a divinely ordained priority of men over women were right.

My fears were unfounded. At the end of six months David and I jointly authored a sixty-page single-spaced report of what we had discovered, along with our conclusions. Writing this paper marked the beginning of our commitment to share equally in the joys and sorrows, the gifts and responsibilities of life with each other and our children. We began teaching classes and leading workshops on the Bible and women, helping spread the good news about men and women as equal partners in life. We worked at making our own relationship more equitable. I believed with all my heart that I had resolved my gender issues.

But I hadn't yet made a connection between my gender and what it meant for me to become a theologian. I thought I could become a theologian without undue reference to gender. I had experienced the unfairness and injustices of growing up female, but I didn't see how that was directly connected to my identity as a theologian. I wanted to be a theologian the way men were theologians. I wanted to do what they were doing at least as well as they did, if not better.

Becoming a theologian seemed mostly a matter of joining intellect with a faithful heart. Being female simply added another angle, or at most a manageable challenge. It didn't seem to affect the process at a basic level. I knew men and women are different, but I assumed we had all been given the same stuff with which to work. It hadn't yet dawned on me that growing up female had left me with a set of experiences, attitudes and expectations that often differed from those of my male colleagues. I still thought I should be able to do whatever they did, in the same way and according to the same general plan.

Ironically, I minimized the importance of my gender even as I worked hard to demonstrate that it was OK for me to be studying theology and working on an equal-partnership marriage. As I saw it, my early attention to biblical and theological issues regarding women in church and society was necessary but preliminary. It was a way of clearing the decks, ridding myself of false impediments. Once this was accomplished I could get on with the real stuff of theology—the things male theologians wrote and talked about. I would learn their language so I could join in their conversations. My theology would be as sound as any man's theology. In fact, I expected that as I became a theologian my gender would fade into the background. I would finally be part of the club.

During my final year of seminary my systematic theology professor spoke frequently about the need for women to teach systematic theology. He encouraged me, along with other women, to consider this calling. He said it wouldn't be easy and we should count the cost before setting out.

I didn't have a clue how costly it would be. When two other professors also urged me to consider seminary teaching, I decided to apply for graduate studies. I knew I enjoyed theological studies. I would decide about teaching if such a possibility ever arose. But I was sure there would be no teaching position anywhere for an evangelical feminist theologian who was married, with two children, and nearly forty.

When I began doctoral studies I left behind the freeing evangelical atmosphere of seminary. Without warning, being an evangelical feminist became a problem, a puzzle to be commented on. It was great that I was a feminist; how could I also be evangelical? Gender didn't seem to be a stumbling block. I didn't have to argue that women belong in graduate school studying theology. Nonetheless, I felt bound. Only part of my identity as a woman theologian was actively celebrated.

To make matters more complex, I discovered I didn't know what to do with my evangelical identity. I didn't know any evangelical feminists who had gone through what I was going through. I had deliberately chosen a nonevangelical setting for my doctoral work. Now I wasn't sure what to do with my evangelical commitments.

In this setting evangelicals weren't considered exciting or creative scholars worthy of serious attention. I felt pressured to join in polite but pointed disparagement of most evangelical theologies. Along with several evangelical student colleagues, all white males, I was an exception that proved the rule. Just as I had felt pressure in seminary to distance myself from radical feminists while retaining my feminism, I now felt pressure to distance myself from evangelical theology while retaining my evangelical commitments. My professors, all white males, were kind and affirming, but I often felt trapped and unsure of myself. I managed my discomfort by focusing on research and doing my homework diligently. I chose research topics carefully to fulfill the requirements of my courses and looked for areas of overlapping interest between my professors and me. I didn't want to rock any boats or get into any theological showdowns. Most of all, I didn't want to be forced to choose between evangelicalism and feminism. Despite my vigilance, I feared being co-opted by nonevangelical agendas, thus making myself unacceptable within evangelical circles.

I survived as part of an amazing community of women in my graduate program and the university's divinity school. I was a minority not just because I was evangelical but also because I was married with children. Somehow that didn't matter. We were women committed to women, women meeting regularly to share stories and strategies for survival, women making an impact on the life of our academic community and the church. Though we weren't always in theological agreement, these friends nurtured my feminism, supported me emotionally and celebrated my work.

Meanwhile, back in my doctoral program I still wanted to belong to the club. I was grateful to the women's community for emotional support, and I listened eagerly to every female guest lecturer who visited campus. But I didn't consciously look to these women for academic or intellectual modeling. Even if there had been evangelical feminist theologians available to me as models or mentors, I don't know that I would have done anything differently. I was still intent on becoming a theologian the way men become theologians. I used gender to organize much of my research, and I read feminist theologians in depth. But ultimately I wanted to become worthy of the male network that would someday support my theological work and affirm me as a theologian.

Ironically, though my professors and friends supported my feminism during these years, I didn't look deeply into the significance of my gender. My work remained at a somewhat abstract level, dealing with theological issues concerning women generally. I was still coming to terms with myself as *a* woman, not yet ready to face what it meant to be *this* woman with *these* ties. Perhaps my discomfort about being evangelical was God's invitation to begin looking at this tie that was obviously binding me. In retrospect, I don't think so. In any case, I wasn't ready to respond—not because of disinterest in my evangelical identity but because other more deeply rooted ties needed to be examined first.

Leaving graduate school to teach in a seminary was a shock to my system. I couldn't believe there was an evangelical seminary that wanted a woman to teach systematic theology. I also couldn't believe how difficult teaching was. My students and I barely survived our first year together.

During those early months and years I was often asked to tell my story. How was it that a young girl from a conservative Christian family ended up going to graduate school and teaching systematic theology? Surely I had experienced opposition from my family of origin. Back then I knew only one way to answer the question. Repeatedly I pointed with gratitude to the positive legacy I had inherited. Love of theology ran deep in my family, as did appreciation for academic achievement and service to the church. My parents were proud of what I had accomplished. As I saw it then, all opposition to me as a woman had come from outside my family and from my own fears and self-doubt.

I inherited from my family a rich and positive legacy that has served me well as a theologian. Nonetheless, the ties that have bound me most painfully are also part of my family inheritance.

They are deeply connected to my gender. I'm not just a woman. I'm the firstborn in *this* family, the eldest child of *this* mother and *this* father, the oldest of *these* four daughters, one of many women in a large extended family with *this* history. Coming to terms with myself as a woman theologian has meant coming to terms with myself as *this* woman theologian.

I've been bound by the need for male approval longer than I can remember. I didn't do this to myself. The binding began in ways I'll never understand, long before I decided to jump from the tree in my back yard. Certain behaviors and attitudes were rewarded; others were punished. In my family what mattered most wasn't what was going on inside me but what showed on the outside. I turned into my own best police force. I grew up memorizing and playing by the rules in an atmosphere in which men were clearly in charge and had the power and determination to enforce their will. Though I cared what women thought of me, my attention was ultimately on the men in my life. I believed they held the key to my success or failure.

This belief proved costly in my development as a theologian. My search for the approval of men has had a constricting effect. Because I believed I needed the approval of male professors and colleagues, I tried to make my theological agenda fit into or at least complement their agendas. I was bound more to my projections of what men would find theologically interesting than to my own theological interests. Sometimes I formed conclusions about what would be important by talking things over with significant men in my life. More often, however, I've gone crazy in my mind trying to figure out on my own what would be considered significant and worthy of attention. At times, as in the writing of my dissertation, most of the pieces came together. But often I found myself floundering, looking for direction externally rather than internally. I tried to guess what would be interesting enough to maintain my energy, without requiring me to move outside a range of topics and viewpoints I thought would be at least tolerable to male theologians in my life.

Actually there have been far more significant women than men in my life. More women than men have cared for and about me as I've become a theologian. But I haven't been bound to them in the ways I've been bound to men. This too has been costly.

On the day I jumped from the tree, I knew my mother was in the kitchen. But it didn't occur to me to talk with her about my dilemma. I assumed the challenge had been issued and it was time to put up or shut up. I didn't entertain other points of view. I wasn't aware there were other points of view—not just about whether I needed to jump from the tree but about what jumping meant or didn't mean for me as female.

Over the years I've missed the good counsel of scores of good women. Though I admired and respected them, I was bound in ways I still don't understand by my need for male approval.

Attending to what it means to be *this* theologian has led inexorably to race. My family is white. We are part of the history of white people in the United States of America. My need for male approval has been a need for *white* male approval. Like gender, whiteness binds me in ways I don't understand, ways entrenched long before I was born. Yet unlike gender, it worked in me for years as an invisible binding. No one punished or humiliated me because I was white. Nor did I long to be nonwhite the way I sometimes longed to be male.

As a theologian I avoided what it means that I'm a white woman by focusing on issues I thought concerned all women and by thinking of myself as simply *a* woman rather than *this* woman. My race was an accident of history over which I had no control and for which I thus bore no particular responsibility. It was part of the air I breathed. Since I wasn't intentional about choosing whiteness and it didn't seem to disrupt my life, I didn't need to be intentional about investigating it with reference to myself or my theology. I resented white people who, over several decades, regularly invited me to examine my racism.

In my theological work I was interested in theologies from women of color, but I didn't yet recognize in their work an invitation for me to reexamine my side of the story. I heard it as their story, not as a story that also shed light on my story. As I looked back at the history of the United States, I absolved myself of responsibility for slavery by pointing to the obvious: I wasn't present when those atrocities were committed. I eased my conscience by splitting myself off from history. I thought I could distance myself from the racial sins of white men and white women. I thought I had the power to declare myself untouched by the sins of past generations. My family had always been kind to black people, especially after we moved to the South. Yes, there was a problem, but it wasn't in me or in my family.

Yet there's a deep connection between the history of my family and the history of my country. The air I breathed in my family helped perpetuate, almost effortlessly, a complex web of familial and racial sin. I've inherited a white legacy of unconscious and conscious racist attitudes. I've also inherited an inclination to play it safe by looking the other way or keeping silent. I've inherited a tendency to blame, punish and humiliate people who are vulnerable. I've also inherited a need to believe I'm not racist.

I once thought that because I'd read all about it, I understood what it means to be white and how racism affects me. Now I'm learning by being caught in the act. Caught in the act of oversight or presumption. Caught feeling uncertain and uneasy about how I'm perceived by nonwhite students, colleagues and friends. Caught needing their approval. Caught behaving and thinking in constricted, fearful ways. Caught hoping someone else will speak up. Caught in ignorance about the myriad ways I've benefited from growing up white and female. Caught unaware of being white in everyday situations of overwhelmingly visible and unfair white advantage.

Becoming a theologian includes beginning the discipline of attending to things we would rather avoid or forget. It means attending not just to particular doctrinal beliefs but to particular corners and rooms in our lives as they begin coming into view. We'll never fully understand ourselves. But we can form the habit of looking inward and backward, using the present crisis, fear, boredom, confusion, blindness, anger or self-destructive habit as a guide to what comes next.

Many seminarians bring heavy loads to their studies, unfinished business that already interferes with their ability to focus. Many come from crisis situations in which they heard a call to ministry. Most want to turn over a new leaf, leave the past behind and look forward to a better tomorrow. They want to help others avoid the pain, betrayal or injustice they've endured. What's true of them is true of many church people. They too want things to be different. They look for churches that won't perpetuate damage done to them. They too want to leave an unhappy or confused past behind.

But becoming a theologian is about remembering the past. It's about discovering movement and direction in seemingly uncon- nected events and stages of life. It's about finding life where there seemed to be only death. This isn't a neat, predictable step-by- step process. Rather, it's like jumping into the middle of a systematic theology, beginning to look around and discovering how everything is connected to everything else.

Life as a theologian has been an ongoing discovery of often surprising ways in which everything in my life is connected to everything else—especially to my identity as a theologian. I can't leave myself outside the door. When I do, I'm no longer becoming a theologian. I'm just thinking about it.

Becoming a theologian means beginning again. It means tak- ing slow, awkward, unfamiliar steps to let go of my need for white male approval. It means establishing new connections with women, children, young people and men. It means being caught in the act of white racism so that I can repent and learn to do things differently. The ability to forgive myself for colluding against the weak and the vulnerable, including myself, is a key to forgiving others. As I have learned this, many people and situations I once feared have become sources of insight and strength.

My body, once ignored and despised, has become an ally in the reorientation of my internal and external life. It lets me know when I'm running away, avoiding yet another of God's invitations to look into my past and the way it binds me as a theologian. I can't trust my mind as often as I can trust my body. My mind tries to talk me into business as usual, but my body isn't fooled. Insomnia, intestinal pain and diarrhea let me know there's work to be done.

As I write this chapter, I hear voices raising objections. Looking into ties that bind is too personal, too subjective, too negative. Wouldn't it be better to focus on the positive? There's no need to dredge up the past or open old wounds. Someone might get hurt. Besides, who has time for this self-centered navel gazing? There are people out there who need our help. How dare we theologians spend time on such self-indulgence while the world is starving to death? We need to *do* something about it instead of getting stuck thinking about ourselves. We can't afford to lose our prophetic edge. Besides, this doesn't sound very productive for the church or for the world. Aren't you just buying into the spirit of the present age, retreating into splendid, self-absorbed isolation?

There's good reason to ask these questions. Attending to ties that bind me as a theologian has disrupted my life and my relationships far more than any disruption my theology might cause in other people. But it hasn't resulted in narrow vision or isolation. On the contrary, accepting God's invitation to stop running from ties that bind me has brought me out of isolation and out of a constricted understanding of myself as a theologian.

While working through these ties to reclaim a blessing, I've dealt directly with people instead of hiding from them. I've read books and gone through family records to discover where and when I entered the larger and smaller history of my family, the church and the nation. But my chief work has been connecting with women, children, young people and men in ways unlike my contacts and avoidances of the past. Attending to these ties has drawn me out of isolation and into my larger communities. It means talking about things I would rather just think about, being open when I would rather be silent and giving up comfortable survival skills that have become destructive. It means testing fears about what I can and cannot do or say, instead of letting fear bind me to safe, tried and untrue behaviors.

God's invitation to stop running from ties that bind is gracious but never gentle. It always feels like the end of the world as I know it. Indeed, it *is* the end of the world as I know it. The end of belief that I'm handling things just fine on my own. The end of my always precarious hope that I've finally figured out how to survive as an evangelical feminist theologian, or as a female theologian married with children. The end of the delusion that I'm untouched by the sins of my white fathers and white mothers. The invitation to rest doesn't come softly and tenderly but with great shocks and jolts to my system, upheavals that bring me face to face with my participation in *human* history.

The upheavals aren't side issues. They aren't unfortunate interruptions to get out of the way so I can get on with the so-called real work of theology. They are, in fact, my work as a theologian. They keep me close to the truth that God hasn't given up on human history. God hasn't abandoned the messiness of our lives in favor of less threatening involvement in a world of ideas. As a theologian I'm called to reflect this engagement of God with human history. And I'm called to reflect it from the inside out, as God does in Jesus Christ, through the Holy Spirit.

3

Theological Commitments

I WAS BORN INTO CHRISTIANITY. Headed by my father, an ordained minister, my family was a churchlike training ground for me and my three younger sisters. From the womb we were immersed in Christian walk and talk. My mother played hymns and choruses on the piano. We had daily family devotions around the dining-room table. We worked hard to remember what we had read from the Bible the day before and then took turns reading aloud the next part of the story. My father led us in long prayers for our extended family and missionaries we knew around the world. My mother, sisters and I prayed too, not nearly as long. We memorized Scripture. We listened to moral lessons spelled out in stories about farm animals my father had known. We went to church a lot. We listened to my father's sermons. And we were punished regularly for sins of omission and commission.

Christianity was a way of life, not a choice. It was an infinitely superior way, though my friends down the road seemed to be having a lot more fun than I was. Though it was a sin, I was proud of being good and thus superior. Even as I envied them, I pitied my friends who were clearly flirting with the broad road that leads to destruction.

Were the people who crossed our path *real* Christians? This question seemed to hover around every encounter not just outside church but within it. Signs of perhaps less than total Christian dedication were sorrowfully noted. "I understand he's been through a divorce." "I think one of her children is in trouble with the law." They seem so nice; it's such a shame. Maybe we can help them.

None of this seemed overtly based on doctrine, though we talked a lot about God and the Bible. I don't remember theological debates or being introduced to the finer points of doctrinal correctness. I just remember the call to right behavior, backed up when necessary by appeals to what the Bible teaches. I remember daily exhortations about being obedient, modest, cheerful, considerate of others and a good example not simply to my younger sisters but to the entire world. We were separated from the world by a strict behavioral code and the conviction that the world was watching us.

We belonged. We were insiders. *Real* Christians. Many who claimed to be Christian were not. We were vigilant lest we be seduced from the true and narrow way. Looking and acting differently was supposed to add a layer of protection.

Ironically, the world which seemed a constant threat rarely intruded on our family life. School and church friends were our major source of information about how other families lived. Our few family friends who seemed outrageously worldly were constant reminders of what we were to avoid. The rest of the time a long list of prohibitions kept the world at bay: no movies, no cards, no dancing, no swearing, no Sunday newspaper funnies until Monday morning.

Theological commitment was nurtured in me from day one, as commitment not to right doctrine but to right behavior.

Behavior was the single most important determining factor for belonging to the Christian tradition. Anyone could claim to believe certain doctrines; few had the life to prove it. Being committed to this way of life merged imperceptibly into belonging to the family. Openly questioning or rejecting the rules would have been like leaving the family—not belonging anymore, not having a theological *or* familial home.

I've ached to belong ever since I was old enough to feel left out. The process of becoming a theologian didn't remove the ache. Rather, it intensified it. Becoming a Christian theologian is about belonging to the Christian tradition, finding a theological home.

Over the years many voices, each speaking in God's name, have offered solutions to my inner longing: join us, and you'll truly belong! Belonging meant giving assent to a set of theological commitments. Holding them close. Guarding them. Investigating and defending them. Living them out. Talking about them a lot. Making sure I used the right language and knew the crucial code words and behaviors. It meant being alert, since certain other theological commitments were dangerous, naive, even un-Christian.

When I was sixteen I left home for Bible college. I traveled 150 miles only to discover that Bible college was an extension of my home, a training ground for young white Christian ladies and gentlemen. I felt strangely liberated even as I submitted to these men and women who had my best interests at heart. I welcomed the many rules that made decisions easy. Sometimes I felt I had died and gone to heaven. Never before had I been in a large community of so many like-minded believers. Exceptions stood out like sore thumbs, reinforcing the rightness of this more excellent way.

At Bible college belonging meant submitting rather than rebelling. It meant keeping all the rules, in the right spirit, thereby gaining the admiration and approval of men and women in authority over me. It meant learning the biblical and theological beliefs of my teachers and not asking too many questions. It meant agreeing with my Bible and theology professors that women weren't created for heavy-duty theological investigation or for leadership over men. It meant accepting responsibility as women for the moral climate of the campus. Our deans exhorted us regularly to be vigilant lest one of us cause the men to stumble in thought, word or deed. In my desire to belong to this institution which seemed to possess truth and a way of life the rest of the world desperately needed, I gave my full consent.

When I graduated from Bible college I was prepared for life. At college I met and became engaged to a man who shared my theological commitments. He also welcomed and respected my intelligence. A year after my graduation we married. My family was delighted; their eldest daughter was safely on her way.

Two weeks and about a thousand miles later I woke up in a strange land, totally unprepared for the first year of our marriage. It was a cruel shock. With a few gracious exceptions, people we met didn't know how to treat me. Some didn't even make eye contact. Their excitement upon meeting David only underscored their awkwardness around me. Marriage seemed to have stripped me of my former identity as musician, intelligent conversationalist, college graduate and valued lay worker.

I had a wonderful secretarial job that helped support us while David began graduate studies. But outside my job I didn't belong to any group that recognized me as more than David's wife and the potential mother of his children. In the long winter evenings I often stood for hours staring out the window, watching wrecked cars being towed into the garage across the street from our apartment. Sometimes I sat immobile on the sofa, watching David read books and write papers.

In the second year of our marriage I was offered a position as organist and choir director in a neighborhood Presbyterian church. I accepted eagerly. Perhaps becoming involved in music again would ease some of my need to be known and to belong, especially within a church. We decided to join the church and attended classes for new members. I wasn't particularly concerned about understanding the Reformed theology of the Presbyterian church. My family background was a mixture of conservative Christianity and Reformed piety. I felt enough at home to give assent without much study of what it meant to be Presbyterian. Besides, my husband had joined the Presbyterian church when he was a teenager. Surely he knew best. Becoming Presbyterian seemed the natural thing for us to do.

During the next several years I flourished as church musician and gave birth to our first child. My depression of our first year of marriage seemed to have vanished.

We moved back to the Bible college, where David began teaching full time. I began mothering full time. Before the end of our first year we had joined another Presbyterian church, David had been ordained a ruling elder, and I had given birth to our second child. We became cosponsors of the youth group and helped produce a few wild talent shows. I still hadn't looked seriously at what it means to be Presbyterian. I didn't have time. I was busy living out my theological commitment to being a good wife and mother. The stakes were high. Faculty wives were living examples of the Bible college way of family life. I still considered myself a model student.

My depression returned. This time I didn't have hours to spend staring out the window at other people's lives. I wept inconsolably. My husband had a life; I didn't. I loved my children and I loved my husband. I was keeping all the rules. And I was miserable. Well-meaning female friends sympathized and said things would get worse. I should get down on my knees daily and thank God for the privilege of being married to this wonderful man whom God was going to use mightily. I was devastated.

Several months later I turned to a Christian counselor. She told me I needed to go home and resubmit myself to my husband. By now I was willing to try anything. I went home and tearfully made my confession to David: I had lost my willingness to be a submissive wife. Surely these were the right words about the right behavior. But David didn't buy them.

Together we began turning a corner. As it turned out, what wasn't working for me wasn't working for David either. Four years after returning to the Bible college, we moved on.

And so nearly ten years after graduating from college, I moved with my family to the West Coast and enrolled in seminary. Besides my unexamined Presbyterian identity, I brought with me disillusionment about the Bible college way of life. I felt trapped in a theological worldview that didn't seem to care how I felt or what my calling might be, beyond the undeniably crucial work of mothering our children.

In the evangelical commitments of my seminary I found another way. I didn't yet understand what it meant to be evangelical, but I began to feel at home. The seminary actively supported women in ministry, whether married or single. Christian belief and Christian behavior were valued as harmonious accompaniments of professional excellence. Commitment to the church included rigorous scholarship. Belonging was about pursuing knowledge and gaining academic skills that would enhance ministry in the church and open doors to wider academic discourse. Belonging meant coming of age academically and professionally. It meant becoming a product the seminary would be proud of.

Given my academic gifts and hunger for something more, I immersed myself in seminary studies willingly and gratefully. Here was water for a thirsty female soul, water for which I had longed all my life. In this setting I first understood how the gospel of Jesus Christ is indeed living water.

Although I didn't fully realize it then, I paid a price. Immersing myself in seminary meant immersing myself in the academic world of evangelicals. This world had an agenda already set and dominated by certain issues and certain theologians. Seminary provided tools that enabled me to join the conversation already in progress. It encouraged me to speak out from time to time, especially on matters concerning women. I worked diligently to make sure my contributions fit into, spoke to, elaborated upon, enhanced understanding of or accepted in some way the agreed-upon agenda. I was grateful to be included. Women who chose another way or raised other agendas weren't even at the table. I didn't want to be known as one of "them." I needed to belong. I calculated my contributions prudently, modulating my voice lest I appear too strident.

In my third year of seminary I decided to pursue further graduate training in theology. My systematic theology professor reviewed the options with me. I had never studied in a liberal theological setting or been in a secular university. If I was going to teach systematic theology, it might be wise to get my feet wet in different waters.

The prospect terrified me. Nothing in my family, church or Bible college background had prepared me for this possibility. On the other hand, seminary training had equipped me well for the rigors of doctoral work. It had also given me a major dose of Protestant evangelical theology. I sent off my application forms, halfway hoping I wouldn't be accepted. But I was. Following six months of language study in Germany and one last course at the seminary, I moved with my family and our cat across country yet again.

Beginning doctoral work felt like going back to first grade. Overnight I felt like a naive, sheltered, simple-minded believer whose chief redeeming features were commitment to women and to doing my homework. I was in a foreign country, learning to speak a language I had never heard. During my first year of classes I routinely returned home needing to be put back together. Where had I been all my life? Was it humanly possible to do all the remedial reading I felt I needed to do? Why hadn't I heard of these theological issues before? Maybe I had, and I just didn't get the language game yet. Why did my professors keep encouraging me to become more critical of the Christian tradition?

By my second year of coursework I understood what was required if I was to belong to this community of learning. I needed commitment to rigorous theological method, though without appeal to Scripture as a unique foundational source. I needed commitment to open-minded reevaluation of every belief, though not necessarily accompanied by enthusiastic commitment to the Christian church. I would explore and construct theological proposals responsive to the sensitivities and anxieties of the twentieth century. Scholarly excellence would serve the cause of social justice in church and society.

Some of this was familiar and welcome; seminary had prepared me well. As a Reformed Christian feminist I found more than enough space for pursuing doctoral work. But as an evangelical I had different commitments to Scripture and the church. I knew I would never belong fully to this community, though faculty and student colleagues supported me faithfully and encouraged me at every step.

Beginning with my family of origin, every Christian community in which I have lived, worked and worshiped has produced garments for me to wear, sometimes hand-me-downs, sometimes new. Labels abounded: independent conservative, nondenominational mission-oriented, mainline denominational, progressive evangelical, Christian feminist, post-Enlightenment liberal, ecumenical evangelical, social justice activist. It didn't seem to matter who it was: belonging meant putting on *our* garments and wearing them proudly. Some always fit; some always didn't. And even garments that fit always seemed to clash with each other. How could this be?

Over the years I kept hoping to discover a set of theological commitments that fit. In my fondest dreams some other theologian, movement or organization would hand me an identity that would clarify once for all how I belong to the Christian tradition. All the pieces would finally come together, giving me a theological home.

Meanwhile I needed a way of identifying myself theologically. How would I connect myself to the Christian tradition that ran like a thread through *all* these theological approaches? I drew on a survival skill nurtured in me from childhood and modeled at every stage of my so-called higher education: I developed the fine art of belonging on the outside. No matter where I found myself, I took up a position on the outside, withholding myself from full membership. I became a critical presence, owning my relationship to Christianity by way of *disowning* its many failures and limitations. Strangely, no matter where I went I found myself surrounded with like-minded individuals. Lonely, but not alone.

It was easy to operate as a critic. Given my background, this supposedly scholarly habit of the mind and heart felt more than comfortable. It felt right. And if I wasn't as critical of the Christian tradition as my doctoral professors would have liked, I had little hesitation about being critical of them.

By the time I began teaching at an American Baptist seminary, I had developed sharp analytical skills and a wondrous ability to point out exactly what the other person had failed to say or places where the other person's logic simply didn't hold up. And though I was interested in knowing other theologians' contexts, my goal was usually to explain why they were biased in unhelpful ways or why they had failed to see what I saw.

Perhaps some of this needed to be said. Nevertheless, what

was missing was a sense of common ground. Not common doctrinal ground, but common *human* ground. Awareness that my own theological efforts were as flawed and limited as the other person's.

It's deceptively easy not to belong to the Christian tradition, especially when we're becoming theologians. There's so much we wish hadn't happened, so much we don't want to perpetuate, so much that has caused pain and death. We distance ourselves lest anyone think we could be guilty of falling into the same egregious errors. We wouldn't want anyone to think we're blind to the many failures and shortcomings of Christianity and the Christian church.

It was dangerous and painful remaining on the outside, but I thought I belonged there. God had called me to this seemingly prophetic position on the outside looking in. I became committed to speaking from what I believed to be God's perspective, handing down judgments and studiously careful analysis of what was wrong with Christianity.

But somewhere along the way, in my desire to speak for truth and against falsehood, I forgot I was part of the system. I had discovered how to keep showing up without actually belonging. I was lost.

I can't document a day and time when the change began. Rather, I went through a series of awakenings initiated by crises in my personal life. This spilled over into reexamination of myself as theologian. I didn't leave my former self behind. There weren't any dramatic overnight transformations. Yet over time I came to a new way of seeing myself in relation to the Christian tradition.

For years I'd known I could never divest myself of the Christian tradition. Even in my most critical moments I knew I was talking about a tradition that had somehow nurtured me. Yet only in this conversionlike process did I begin to understand. I don't just stand *within* the tradition; the tradition stands inescapably within *me*.

Becoming a theologian is like deciding to look into family history. It's an acknowledgment that I'm already part of this tradition and am willing to take a closer look—not just because of what I'll learn about the tradition but because of what I'll learn about myself. To attempt this without a sense of belonging for good and for ill is like treating my family history as though it were another family's history. Or pretending to have an academic rather than a personal stake in the outcome. It's like being a spectator rather than a full participant. An armchair critic. A customer hoping to find a better bargain.

In the process of becoming theologians God invites us to belong to the Christian tradition, to find ourselves at home. Belonging means being known as "one of them," instead of distancing ourselves out of shame, embarrassment or disappointment. It means actively looking into the Christian tradition, especially the parts that most trouble us. It means no longer thinking of ourselves as superior exceptions to the rule. It means celebrating the gifts we've received instead of being stingy with our gratitude. It means joining the conversation as full partners instead of remaining silent for fear of what others might think. It means beginning to understand where and when we entered this picture that is larger than all of us put together. Belonging to the Christian tradition is about being willing to be seen in the picture. All of it—the good, bad, ugly, tragic, beautiful, graceful Christian picture.

I'm part of the system, the very system upon which I felt called to make constant corrective comment. I don't belong on the outside looking in with a critical eye but on the inside looking around, counting on God to open my eyes. Belonging is about taking time to let my eyes adjust to the dark so that I can begin to see what I've been missing, including the light.

I felt awkward and uncertain when I first began thinking about these things. Most of my training had been along the lines of constant critical comment. I remembered a few teachers and professors who didn't do things this way. But the vast majority seemed to have thrived precisely because they remained somewhere on the edges, pointing out clear and present dangers to the rest of us—or trying to redirect traffic.

I wanted to change. Indeed I had to change. But I wasn't sure where to begin. I knew I couldn't erase everything and start over with a blank slate, though I wished I could. Nor could I in one human lifetime look into every nook and cranny of the Christian tradition. I could only go at this the way I was learning to go at the rest of my life, piece by piece.

I decided to begin with my present theological identity. That's where I live as a theologian most of the time. What does it mean to be Protestant, Reformed, a member of the Presbyterian Church (U.S.A.), a North American evangelical, a white Christian feminist? For years I had checked off all these boxes when asked about my theology. Now I had to face the reality that some were more attractive and easier to own than others. I understood some pieces better than others. Remedial work was in order.

In the process of learning more about my present identity I found courage to begin looking into my past. What did I inherit theologically the day I was born? How did it shape not just my personal identity but my theological identity? I knew that in my haste to leave behind parts of that heritage, I had jettisoned entire sets of luggage without taking time to examine their contents. What did they contain? Had I really left all this behind? Did I want to reclaim anything?

I belong to the Christian tradition only by way of these sometimes jarring pieces of my theological identity. From time to time I've ignored or neglected some of them, hoping to discover a more exciting place in the Christian tradition or a more easily understood identity. But my goal isn't to understand exactly how all the pieces fit together. It's to discover bit by bit how these theological commitments already connect me to the larger picture. I know it's working, because already I'm finding myself more at home, leaving some of my awkwardness and uncertainty behind.

Beginning with my present theological identity and looking into my theological past simplifies everything. It frees me from the awful paralysis of trying to figure out what to do next or what might be interesting or significant to someone else. I must do this work myself in order to take my place in the Christian picture. No one else can do it for me. It also frees me from the need to look into and say something about everything other people would like to place on my agenda. I used to be plagued by guilt when friends asked my opinion about lectures, books, demonstrations, articles or forums I hadn't attended or read. Now the moment of guilt usually passes quickly. I'm busy with other work.

Best of all, by attending to my particular theological identity I've begun to join the greater cloud of Christian witnesses. Belonging to the Christian tradition isn't just about investigating doctrinal themes. My early family training pointed me in a good direction. Belonging to the Christian tradition is about behavior. It's about how I treat my theological neighbors near and far. It's about taking time to know them one by one, listening to them, learning what motivates, excites and infuriates them. It's about becoming known. And it's about finding myself in a place of encouragement, hope, strength, repentance and sobriety.

When I was growing up, being different meant not belonging. For years I tried to make myself fit into the picture by pointing to my clear connections to the Christian tradition. Anything that stood out as different seemed suspect, and I became skilled at determining when to minimize the differences. I lived in fear of being judged unworthy. This or that piece of my theological identity would have to go; it just didn't, wouldn't, couldn't fit.

Now I'm learning to wear my theological identity as a garment that fits *me*. Being different isn't an impediment. It's part of belonging, part of life. I'm learning to be connected *and* different rather than connected *but* different. I'm learning to stand up straight and look right into the camera with a big smile on my face.

4

Befriending
the Bible

WHEN I WAS ELEVEN YEARS OLD I graduated from seventh grade.
Dressed in white, I sat with my classmates on the platform in the
chapel of our Presbyterian church day school. I received honors
not just for good grades but for my accomplishments in Bible
classes. Many of my classmates and I had dutifully memorized
lists of kings and apostles plus entire chapters of Scripture.
Studying the Bible was as normal as studying arithmetic. So was
carrying our Bibles to school.

Directly across the street from our grade school was a public
junior-high school. I had eyed this imposing, graceless red brick
structure for the last six years. It seemed an alien world, popu-
lated by worldly teenagers who had not the least desire to study
the Bible. I watched them arriving and departing daily on yellow
buses, smoking on the sly, making loud and boisterous remarks
to each other, sometimes fighting. Whenever they yelled across
the street at us, I turned away quickly, burning with fear and
inexplicable shame.

During the summer of my graduation from seventh grade I

was assigned to attend eighth grade at this junior high. I was horrified. I determined to survive by being inconspicuous and diligent. But what about my Bible? Was I going to continue carrying it to school? Leaving it home didn't seem the Christian thing to do. I wanted to give a clear Christian witness. Besides, what would my family and my friends at church think? I resolved to carry it to school. But exactly how would I carry it? And what would I do with it after I got there? I fought an impulse to arrange it underneath my other books. That would work well only if the other books were smaller than my Bible.

I arrived at school. Maybe I didn't have to leave my Bible out in full view right on top of my desk. Nonchalantly and expeditiously, I deposited it in the compartment under my seat. This was a lot more complicated than I had anticipated.

Within several weeks my home-room teacher had helped me rationalize my dilemma by asking me to be in charge of morning devotions. That meant I got to read a Bible passage of my choice every morning before leading the class in the Lord's Prayer. She had a Bible on her desk for just this purpose. I told her I would use my own.

Classmates were curious. Why was I carrying my Bible to school? I explained my need to have it for home-room devotions. When they pointed out the Bible on the teacher's desk, I said I needed to have my own Bible so I could pick out a passage before school began. Sometimes I told them I carried it because I was a Christian. When they pointed to other Christians (often including themselves) who didn't carry their Bibles to school, I didn't know what to say.

One word characterizes my relationship to the Bible for most of my life since the seventh grade: *embarrassment.* What was I going to do with this book that meant so much to me but didn't seem to fit into my everyday life? I loved the Bible. I couldn't imagine life without it. I had grown up in a home where Bible training was as natural as learning to wash the dishes or set the table. By the time I graduated from high school I had assisted my parents in countless children's Bible club meetings and had spent a summer as a junior counselor at a Bible camp. If anything should have come easily to me, it was relationship to the Bible. But when I tried to bring it into everyday life outside my home or church-related settings, I felt strangely separated not just from other people but from the Bible itself. I coped as best I could, soothing myself by remembering my many accomplishments as a student of the Bible.

I expected things to change at Bible college. Several friends had gone to this college, and they seemed very comfortable with the Bible. The Bible college assumed I already had, or was willing to acquire, a personal relationship to the Bible characterized by an attitude of obedient and docile submission.

Every morning the dormitory bell rang for us to get up. Thirty minutes later a second bell rang to signal the beginning of quiet time. For half an hour I sat reading my Bible and praying. Then another bell rang to signal time for breakfast. Bible quotations and Bible exposition permeated classroom lectures, daily chapel services and special meetings. I learned to organize and run neighborhood Bible clubs and developed lesson plans for teaching the Bible. We were required to read the entire Bible through twice before graduation. I was relieved that my quiet time reading counted toward this goal. I didn't have to sit there and figure out what to read next. It seemed the Bible couldn't have been more completely woven into my life.

My growing conviction that I knew the Bible well hid anxiety about my relationship to the Bible. Seeds planted in childhood began to sprout. I was *not* one of those people I later learned to call biblical illiterates. I was different. I had filled my mind with truth, and it was going to pay off for the rest of my life. But a nagging fear remained. I didn't know the Bible as well as people seemed to think I did. Someday they would discover this, along with the secret about my troubled relationship to the Bible.

After graduation from Bible college there were periods in my life when I read the Bible faithfully every day, without bells to regulate my behavior. But most of the time I didn't. Instead I counted on formal Bible study times like Sunday school to keep me in touch with the text. My college had tried to nurture a lifetime habit. I seemed to have developed lifetime guilt. Hearing my friends talk about the wonderful time they'd had "just this morning" reading the Bible only fed my guilt and shame. I felt increasingly separated not simply from the Bible but from my friends as well.

Things began to change when I got to seminary. I studied Greek and Hebrew. I was introduced to commentaries and learned to carry on my own conversation with the text and other interpreters. I discovered that sometimes poor and misleading choices had been made when certain words were translated, especially words that reinforced limited roles and options for women. My professors introduced me to the many cultures within which the biblical texts arose, and I learned to read texts in their cultural context. I discovered the importance of taking seriously every word in the text and of connecting verses with what preceded and followed them.

Gradually I began to hear in the Bible new themes and new ways of talking about life with God. Some harsh edges I had always heard in the Bible softened. I began to lose my fear that the Bible was out to get me. I also lost some of my embarrassment about being seen with it.

When I got to graduate school, however, it seemed my new-found friendship with the Bible would have to be put on hold. Direct appeal to the Bible as an authoritative foundation for theological reflection was discouraged. But my early anxiety proved unfounded. My professors introduced me to the study of interpretation theories. I began to see how particular theories of biblical interpretation work. Some methods focus more on mastering biblical texts by questioning them and analyzing vast amounts of data. Others focus more on making room for biblical texts to question us in their own unexpected ways. My professors also introduced me at breakneck speed to one theologian after another. All these theologians used the Bible, and each of them used it differently.

I watched, sometimes in shock but more often in amazement, as first one insight and then another was uncovered. It had never occurred to me that theological reflection on the Bible might have its own methods and that there might be many ways to go about it. This wasn't simply a continuation of biblical interpretation as I had learned it in seminary.

When I began teaching seminary in 1983 I still didn't have a clear way of interpreting the Bible that would work for me as a theologian. I could exegete specific texts and argue for one interpretation over another. I knew how to deal with Bible texts about women and could work with individual books in the Bible to identify their overarching theological themes. But I didn't yet have a theologically coherent way of reflecting on the Bible as a whole. Nor had I resolved my personal relationship to the Bible. During my first three years of teaching I worked on this task as I wrote my doctoral dissertation and tried to keep up with my students. My major challenge wasn't to get doctrine about the Bible straight. Rather, it was to develop a theological approach that fit my identity as Presbyterian, evangelical, Christian feminist and Bible college graduate from a very conservative family.

I didn't find an answer in a book. Instead, various pieces began coming together, including and going beyond what I had gained from seminary and graduate school. From my family, my Bible college and evangelical theology came an attitude toward Scripture, an attitude of reverence, respect and expectation that God's voice is heard in and through the very words of the Bible—all of them. From feminist theology came commitment to inclusiveness: The Bible is good news for *all* people. It addresses *all* of life. I wanted a method of interpretation accessible to as many people as possible, not just seminary graduates. From my Reformed Presbyterian background came appreciation for the written Word of God as a chief means of grace, and for the necessary work of God's Holy Spirit if I am to experience it as a means of grace. From Jewish scholars working on the Hebrew Scriptures came eyes and ears to appreciate the literary artistry of the Bible's many authors and editors. From Karl Barth came acceptance of my humanity as an interpreter of the Bible and a desire to hear and tell the old story in ways that illumine all our stories.

In my third year of teaching I completed my dissertation on Barth. Dialogue with Barth had been difficult. I didn't agree with his biblical and theological interpretation of what it means to be male and female. Yet the discipline of understanding his arguments from the inside out had opened up ways of hearing the Bible differently, not just in part but in whole.

Out of this seemingly academic exercise I began to reexamine not just my relationships with God and other people but my relationship to the Bible itself. I had always assumed that a more disciplined devotional life or better exegetical skills would somehow fix my relationship to the Bible. Now I began to see that the relationship itself was the point. In fact, my attitudes and patterns of behavior toward the Bible were similar to my attitudes and behaviors toward other people. Most troubling, my expectation that other people would judge me harshly was reflected in the same expectation about the Bible.

I didn't make these discoveries alone. They emerged in conversation with students and friends as we tried to move closer to this book with which many of us had struggled over the years. We all knew the kind of relationship we *didn't* want with the Bible.

But it was difficult to put into words and actions a positive way of relating to it.

I began working with a friend who became my coauthor. Beginning with the assumption that the Bible is primarily a means of grace, we developed a simple process for making friends with the Bible. The process takes seriously the Bible just as it is, what's happening in our lives, and God's freedom to be heard in and through our conversation about the meaning of particular texts.

I never dreamed I would coauthor a book about how I relate to the Bible. In fact, my personal relationship to the Bible had always been a closely guarded secret. As a theologian I was far more comfortable talking about the Bible than carrying on my own conversation with it. I could develop theological themes I heard in the Bible, themes that sometimes brought me to tears. But I didn't know why these themes moved me so deeply, nor could I connect them to what was happening in my life. It was as though the Bible and I lived in parallel worlds, sometimes coming close in ways that evoked deep yearnings in me but never quite connecting around the concrete realities of my everyday life.

Making Friends with the Bible marked a turning point. For the first time in my life I was excited about the Bible: not apologetic or defensive, not guarded and cautious, but totally and irreversibly enthusiastic. Also for the first time I described my relationship to the Bible as I knew it to be instead of trying to fit my experience into someone else's ideas about what this relationship should look like.

Telling the truth was liberating and terrifying. My father and my mother would read *Making Friends with the Bible*. What would they think? Some of my colleagues and former professors who are committed to different interpretive approaches to the Bible might read it. Would they take offense or find me naive? Some of my evangelical friends and some of my feminist friends would read it. Would they find it evangelical enough, or feminist enough? I didn't like being this visible.

I don't relate to the Bible sometimes as a theologian who just happens to be this woman and sometimes as a woman who just happens to be this theologian. My full identity matters. Theological reflection on the Bible isn't disconnected, disinterested examination of the text. It isn't carried out by anonymous individuals on behalf of other anonymous individuals. It isn't about performing prescribed interpretive exercises in order to reach true and absolute conclusions. It isn't even about settling doctrinal disputes. Rather, it's a spiritual exercise in listening. And what I hear is always connected to the worlds in which I live, both internal and external.

Inevitably, theological reflection on the Bible engages others and speaks to questions larger than my own. But this larger work begins with personal time spent with the Bible. Time in which the point of departure is what's going on in *my* life.

If the Bible is a dry well for me personally, it will be a dry well for me theologically. If there's little going on in my relationship to the Bible, there will be little new going on in my theology. I may repeat words that were fresh yesterday, but their connection to what's happening today will be missing. My relationship to the Bible is a touchstone—not because it feeds directly into my theology but because it nurtures life with God and with the people God brings into my life.

What goes around in my life always comes around in my theology. Theological words don't come alive for me until they've passed through this process of personal discovery in which the Bible is a kind of midwife. If I don't know what the Bible's good news looks like in my life, it won't echo in my theology.

I used to think that as a theologian I was expected to come to terms with literally every passage in the Bible. Today I'm grateful for an interpretive approach that supports me as I listen for the good news no matter which passage I'm working on. I don't need to be anxious about getting to the rest. There's more than enough to fill my hunger, past and present. And there's always plenty left over for next time.

My relationship to the Bible is shaped by several basic assumptions about the Bible itself. In fact, befriending the Bible gives me opportunity to discover how these basic assumptions are true. There are four. I'm discovering passage by passage *how* and *to what extent* they're true.

First, I assume the Bible is a mirror, a reflection of what's going on in the world. Not just what happened back then, but what's happening in my world right now. The mirror is made up of clues within the text itself. I can't overlook these clues, especially details I find puzzling, boring or irrelevant. I may need to spend a long time with a text, giving it every benefit of the doubt. Sometimes I may need to put it away for another day. In any case, whenever I begin working on a biblical text I assume it's a mirror that reflects in its own way the truth about what's going on. It tells the truth about life in a fallen world and the truth about God's ways with us in the midst of this world. Recognizing what's happening in the text brings me face to face with what's happening right now. The Bible doesn't present an alien world. It presents a world amazingly like mine, a world into which the light of God's truth is shining in ways that will not be overcome.

Second, I also assume the Bible is primarily a means of grace. There's good news on every page, right from the beginning. This isn't the dubiously good news I heard about when I was growing up. That so-called good news reminded me repeatedly of my many failures and shortcomings. God loved me in spite of my stubborn rebellions. God stood ready to pardon me as soon as I acknowledged from my heart that I deserved the humiliating punishments administered to me in God's name. Only by accepting this bad news could I hope to receive a drop of undeserved good news. But the Bible is a chief means of grace, not a chief means of judgment. I don't know this by reading every page in order to prove it true. Rather, I know this by living with the Bible one passage at a time, especially passages that sound like bad news.

For years I feared difficult passages. They were time bombs waiting to explode, activating voices from my past. The best way to protect myself was to avoid them altogether. Sadly, these time bombs are buried in every page, even those that seem most friendly. There *is* good news on every page of the Bible. There are also voices threatening to drown out the good news. With each text, including those that seem friendly, my worst fears are put to the test. Sometimes these voices try to tell me what the text *has* to mean, especially about me. Or they accuse me of not being like the good and godly person in the text, who is of course closer to the heart of God than I could ever be. The voices point out the many ways I fall short. They cast doubt on the way I'm relating to the text; I probably don't know what I'm doing. Sometimes they sound harmless, even supportive, almost persuasive. They seem to have my best interests at heart. But they do not. Instead they work to destroy my openness to the good news. They try to shut me down under a load of shame, false guilt, despair and humiliation. They are a negative connection to the text. They don't tell the truth about the text, about God, about me or even about my accusers.

Sometimes I talk back to these voices. Sometimes I just turn the corner and leave them standing there.

My third assumption is that the Bible is simultaneously the written Word of God and the words of human witnesses. Not one and then the other, but both together. Unless I take the Bible seriously as the written Word of God, I won't understand the human words of its many witnesses. And unless I take seriously the many words of its human witnesses, I won't understand it as the written Word of God. I can't demonstrate this beforehand. I can only discover it passage by passage as I attend to the details of the text itself. Everything matters. Over the centuries God's Holy Spirit has conveyed grace through *these* words and passages, artfully arranged in *this* order by the Bible's human authors and editors.

I didn't begin to appreciate the Bible as the written Word of God until I began to appreciate it as the words of many human witnesses. I used to think the authors of the Bible were at least partially superhuman. They'd been caught up in a divinely ordered state of mind so that they temporarily lost conscious control of their thoughts. While they were in this altered state, they put into writing what we now call the Bible. I assumed they were all men. There wasn't room in my imagination for texts being passed on orally before being written down.

These men had the status of God. They weren't actually God but had godlike status conferred on them for just this purpose, the recording of God's very thoughts and words. That they lived human lives wasn't very significant. What mattered was their willingness for God to use them as channels, so that we would have a record of everything God wanted us to know. The Holy Spirit somehow lifted them above the rest of humanity. What they recorded was of the same order as what God inscribed on tablets of stone at Mt. Sinai.

Though they used ordinary human words, their words were elevated to the realm of the extraordinary. They occupied a slot reserved just for them. No human words in any other books had been granted the same status. These words were untouchable. True, there were several versions of these human words. Some of my teachers assured me that the best translations are very close to the Greek and Hebrew texts, even though we don't have the original manuscripts. I placed enormous trust in the many scribes who faithfully and painstakingly copied every word for our benefit. Accidental errors weren't cause for alarm. God's Holy Spirit had made sure there were no errors of great import.

Befriending the Bible has meant accepting the humanity of its many authors and editors. They were human beings created, found and kept by God. Like us, they were learning what it means to trust God and how to get along with each other in a fallen world. Like us, they were invited to accept their human limitations as part of God's good order in this world. Like us, they couldn't survive alone. They too were limited by their need for human companions. Their experience of life was limited, as was their understanding. They had limited power and patience, limited wisdom and ability to communicate, limited influence and limited days on this earth.

I grew up thinking my human limitations were weaknesses to apologize for and to get beyond. Furthermore, all signs of fallenness were avoidable in the future if only I put my hand to the plow and didn't look back. Not only did I misunderstand the humanity of the Bible's authors, I misunderstood my own humanity. I thought they were in a protected realm above it all, and I was down here below it all, struggling just to get to first base. I assumed they, like Mary, had been chosen for their exalted work because of their near perfection. Being selected as special messengers for God was simply an affirmation of their superhumanity.

And so the Bible wasn't just the written Word of God but the Word of God written down by superhuman beings. Having these words picked up and delivered in sermons that sounded like my father's stern exhortations to us girls was like having the whole choir deliver God's judgment on my shameful and deficient humanity as I sat cowering in the front row. There was no escape. Every voice seemed to say the same thing. It was all aimed in my direction, punctuated by earnest, well-timed reminders that this was *God's* word, not mere human opinion or mere human interpretation.

I didn't begin to hear good news on every page until I began appreciating the human voices of the authors and editors of the Bible. Their carefully crafted lines matter. They are faithful human witnesses to God and to God's ways not simply with us but with them. Moving closer to them and their worlds, through their many writings and compositions, moves me closer to God, to myself and to my present neighbors. Best of all, if God can convey life through their human witness, God can convey life through my own. Through the centuries God's Holy Spirit has taken up their words, limited and fallen as the authors were, breathing life into and through them. This too is a witness—not to the perfection or godlike status of these authors or their words, but to God's goodness and the adequacy of their human words. Their words are good enough.

None of this works for me without one more basic assumption. The Bible is a unity, a unified witness. Again, I don't know this because I've mastered the entire canon and observed how each part contributes to the whole. Rather, in conversation around particular texts I'm finding out descriptively *how* it is a unity. I'm discovering unity that already exists, larger and more complex than my mind will ever grasp. The intentional, literary artistry of the Bible's many human authors and editors is a sign of its unity. They are a many-voiced chorus of witnesses to the one true God whose character is displayed on every page.

The unity of the Bible isn't destroyed by differences between voices. It can't be manufactured by the imposition of one voice pretending to speak for other voices. Nor is it negated because some witnesses have been considered more reliable than others or because we don't have the original manuscripts. Rather, in and through the limited, fallen humanity of the Bible's many human witnesses, God's Holy Spirit works to make God's character known through the seemingly small details of seemingly unrelated texts.

Discovering the unity of the Bible just as it is goes hand in hand with discovering the unity of my life. I haven't had a sweeping vision that definitively placed every part of my life in perspective. Rather, I've been discovering unity piece by painful piece as I bring different parts of my story into dialogue with passages in the Bible. Things I never understood before, things I've always dismissed as trivial, things I wish hadn't happened to me, things I wish I hadn't done, things in my life that always seemed contradictory—all of this and more is coming into graciously unified focus as I discover the graciously unified witness of the Bible.

As we become theologians, God invites us to make peace with the Bible. This means more than finding a way to coexist peacefully. It means discovering a way to *live* with it. Friendship with the Bible can't be absorbed secondhand or discovered at the end of an exegetical exercise on the text. It's a sink-or-swim approach. You're in or you're out. There's no room for standing on the sidelines waiting to be convinced of everything before jumping in. The attraction of friendship with the Bible isn't academic. It's personal. It begins with the heart in a way that already includes mind and body. And it's persuasive, especially for those of us who know we're needy, who are finding in its pages life and grace for which we've hungered since our birth.

We don't need to spend our lives making sure the "right" words, in the "right" order, are on each page of the Bible. This isn't our task. We're called to friendship with the Bible. We acknowledge that in and through these very human words in *many* human versions God's Holy Spirit administers grace and brings hope alive in places of despair and death. We also acknowledge that death and despair still come at the hands and voices of those of us who use the Bible for our own purposes, knowingly and unknowingly. We may never be entirely comfortable being seen with this friend.

But the Bible's reputation isn't my biggest challenge. My biggest challenge is to keep telling the truth about my relationship to the Bible. This means being concrete and specific, not just when I'm doing personal work on a text but in group Bible study. I must risk describing what I hear in the text and why *these* words ring true at *this* time of my life.

Telling the truth also means admitting I can't understand the Bible by myself. I must be as ready to listen to others as I am to speak.

Finally, it means being honest about the details of the text. My memory is as limited as my understanding. It pays to keep an open book along with an open mind. We're accountable not just to each other and to God but also to the carefully chosen words around which we gather expectantly.

5

Reading
Theological
Texts

I GREW UP BELIEVING CHRISTIAN BOOKS and authors were safe, just like Christian families. There were Christian books all over our house: missionary biographies for children and adults, missionary stories, hymnbooks, chorus books, commentaries, theological books, devotional guides, an occasional Christian novel, and books of instruction for young Christian girls. The latter were like magnets. To my protected eyes (no movies, no TV), this was hot stuff about hot topics like dating and how babies are conceived and how to make sure I didn't get pregnant before I was married. I read these pink-bound books furtively, listening for my mother or father's footsteps coming my way, quickly putting them back exactly as I had found them.

Also lying around the house were plenty of so-called secular storybooks for children: Dr. Seuss creations, the adventures of Babar and Mrs. Babar, Cinderella and her prince, *The Little Red Hen* and *The Poky Little Puppy*. As we grew, we were introduced to Aesop's fables, Brer Rabbit in his briar patch, Peter Pan and Wendy, Nancy Drew, the Hardy Boys, *Little Women* and *Little Men*.

Everyone in the family read books. My sisters and I joined the public library at the earliest possible age.

Reading was my competitive sport. I was proud to be called a bookworm. In the summers I joined the library's reading club. I loved watching the number of books I'd read climb steadily on the chart in the children's reading room. Even more rewarding was returning to school and discovering I'd read more books than my rivals. Reading was both a comfort and a little work of righteousness. It set me apart from most of my classmates and friends. If my summer travels to Bible camps and conferences didn't sound as exciting as going to Bermuda, I could always say I had read a lot of books.

Early in adolescence I discovered there was a greater blessing if my parents and friends at church saw me reading something like *Pilgrim's Progress*. It was also reassuring. Christian books of this caliber wouldn't lead me astray. If I followed their advice and the examples of their heroes and heroines, I too would be happy and avoid heartbreak. I would learn to have good clean fun. Purity of heart and body were directly related to what I put into my mind. No trash in, no trash out.

I read without ceasing all the way through high school. This included plenty of "secular" books. Of course I always read these with distinct reservations. The characters who inhabited these pages were doing the best they could, but if God were in their lives they would be spared a lot of anguish. They would also clean up their language. Their stories were often riveting, but I knew better than to fall into the misguided belief that their lives were exemplary. In the end this "non-Christian" literature simply reinforced my need to believe in and defend the superiority of our family's way of life.

But at Bible college the awful truth I had already begun to suspect was confirmed: Christian books aren't necessarily safe. When I was a child, certain adult books were kept under lock and key at the pubic library. Locks and keys weren't necessary at the Bible college library, since overtly dangerous Christian books never made it onto the shelves at all. Nonetheless, we were warned about the relative dangers of other books that *had* made it. In some ways they were worse, since they mixed truth with error.

One of my professors favored a scheme whereby he and other faculty members would place color codes on book spines to indicate degrees of danger. The plan wasn't approved, but the point was made. Danger that used to lurk in the non-Christian world now lurked subtly within the Christian world and needed to be exposed.

Although I arrived at Bible college prepared for this way of thinking, this was my formal introduction into what I later called danger theology. This theological approach majors on guarding against the dangers of various theological approaches or insights. One of the most efficient ways to avoid these dangers was to avoid books that might entice me toward the brink. I was to look into such books only cautiously and critically, fully armed to do battle. Sometimes we were warned about particular books. Most of the time we just had to be on guard.

Years later, in my very first semester of seminary, I was shocked into a different world. My ethics professor gave us an assignment as preparation for class discussion of pornography. First we had to go into the local adult bookstore and purchase one piece of literature. Then we were to take it home and examine it. Finally we were to report what we discovered, not simply in the reading material but in ourselves.

It was a bold assignment, one that soundly trumped my youthful embarrassment about carrying my Bible to school. I was mortified at the prospect of publicly entering an adult bookstore to purchase what seemed blatantly pornographic literature. One of my few female classmates promised to go with me. Over my gut's loud objections, we carried out the assignment together.

Other seminary assignments seemed tame by comparison. I roamed the library at will, pulled books off the shelves, checked out new ideas and became acquainted with theologians I'd known only by name. I tried to decipher convoluted arguments of centuries past and learned to make distinctions among positions I'd always lumped together. Nothing was off limits.

I read avidly. The seminary library became my second home. The spacious, airy, California light-filled reading room accurately reflected the opening of my mind to vast stores of wisdom and knowledge. Inspired by the outstanding collection of books in the library stacks and by my husband's long-established habit of book buying, I began acquiring books for my personal library. We used freely a generous student discount at the seminary bookstore and combed catalogs for bargains. I began to imagine myself surrounded by shelves and shelves of scholarly books that reflected on the outside the contours of what I was learning on the inside.

Graduate school built upon and enlarged my seminary experience with books. Reading assignments were longer and sometimes more difficult. I was introduced to strange new worlds of meaning that sometimes felt like bizarre worlds of nonmeaning. I struggled to gain facility in new theological vocabulary. I felt overwhelmed by how many books kept coming out in my field. I accepted a job in the divinity school library as student bibliographer in theology. It brought some order to my reading life by paying me to sort through theological journals and publishers' catalogs that I wanted to sort through anyway. So many books and so little time! But I gloried in the struggle and wouldn't trade those years for anything. Not just because of what I learned about books but because of what I began to learn about myself as a reader.

When I arrived at graduate school I was astounded by the way many of my student colleagues asked questions. They had no end of wonderings. One of my female colleagues came to seminars with pages and pages of questions generated by assigned reading. I came with pages and pages of careful notes that recorded little more than the author's arguments and sometimes my beginning critique of the author's position. My notes didn't reflect dialogue with the author. I hadn't explored the author's position in relation to mine. I didn't think I needed to interact with the author or go more deeply into the subject matter. Hadn't the author already done that? There didn't seem much for me to add or ask. My written work depended heavily on exposition and commentary. My professors kept encouraging me to develop my own conversation with authors. I knew what they wanted, but I didn't know how to go about it.

In fact, I had never learned to dialogue with anyone living or dead (as were most authors I was reading). From my childhood, I don't remember open discussion of ideas in which we explored different points of view. At home and at church I could get answers for everything. Seemingly infallible interpretations of life and belief were handed down regularly. They were bolstered by appeals to indisputable facts and the superior knowledge and experience of the authority figure giving the answer, often my father. Questions were entertained, but they became platforms on which certain adults presented their clear answers.

When I was a child, challenging these answers openly was out of the question. Challenging them inwardly felt like ungrateful impertinence. And so I became a rather passive reader, with large assumptions about the author's superior perspective. I didn't take the printed page as an invitation to dialogue or to further discovery. Indeed, as a child and young adult I'd read only a few Christian books that invited me into dialogue. Most seemed written for passive readers such as I—readers who would agree with the author and be grateful for the opportunity to receive such timely instruction.

As I grew older, I sometimes disagreed vehemently with an author. But a sense of futility weighed me down. I was sure nothing would change even if I risked opening my mouth. I regarded most books and articles as self-contained units of information or investigation. Sometimes books and articles seemed to engage each other in conversation, but I didn't think of them as invitations for me to join in, much less to suggest a different approach to the subject matter. I didn't believe my contribution mattered. What mattered was learning what these authors said. The goal of reading was to take in information. Whether I agreed or disagreed was beside the point. Furthermore, opening my mouth to say anything at all would go far beyond my sense of who I was in the arena of theological discourse. I didn't believe that my disagreement *or* agreement could be brought into public discussion as a respectful, worthwhile or valuable point of view.

In graduate school I began turning into a civilized reader. I always thought being civilized meant keeping all the rules. But in this context it meant carrying on conversation as an equal partner in dialogue with an author. On the one hand, it meant learning to give an author the same careful hearing I would like for my words. But more difficult for me, it meant learning to carry on my side of the conversation. I had to let my professors and colleagues know how well I understood an author's point of view. But I also had to make visible my own response, including how the author was inviting me to explore further my own point of view.

Ironically, discovering how to dialogue with theological books brought on a personal crisis. I'd always assumed that reading many theological texts was connected to the acquisition of much knowledge. I fully expected to attain the ideal: female theologian surrounded by a great personal library of books, all of which she has read and remembers and for which she can give a thumbnail sketch and critique on demand.

The crisis had two sides. First, if I spent time dialoguing with an author I couldn't read as many books as I thought I should. Hence I couldn't acquire as much information as I thought I needed to be a theologian. At first this seemed to be a time management problem. In fact it was the surface layer of a deeper personal issue. Thanks to the way I *didn't* interact with books, I had for years avoided facing a truth about myself. The truth is, I'm not a data person. I'd survived thus far thanks to excellent short-term retention of data and the ability to be a passive reader.

I've been uncomfortable owning the truth about my ability to retain data, especially in academic settings where long-term control of data is highly valued. Details matter. I can't function as a theologian without paying attention to details. But I'm not a walking theological encyclopedia. Over long periods I can recall a lot, but only when I've understood it from the inside out, talked or written about it, and gone back as often as needed to refresh my memory. Even then I find angles of vision and important details I've overlooked or forgotten.

For years I didn't recognize this truth about myself. I knew I could usually discover an author's argument and explain it in my own words. And so I also expected myself to retain that understanding, unaided, for a long time. It seemed an intrinsic part of becoming a theologian.

It's freeing to know that my strength isn't retention of large amounts of data. I now concentrate on listening carefully to authors instead of trying to remember everything they say. The point isn't to accumulate vast storehouses of information. It's to understand an author's point of view and engage him or her in conversation.

There was a second side to this crisis. If I spent more time listening carefully to fewer authors, how would I read the many *other* theological books on my agenda? I had to give up reading habits to which I'd clung for years, believing they proved I was a good reader. I don't know where all this nonsense came from. But I had been a good girl for a long time. It took awhile to get beyond feeling that doing things differently meant I was doing it the wrong way. In seminary I'd been introduced to Mortimer Adler's *How to Read a Book*. It was a required text in my biblical interpretation course. Now I took a second look and gained even more appreciation for Adler's perceptive, practical, common-sense insights into reading books for understanding.

I learned from Adler to use seemingly peripheral parts of books: titles and subtitles, indexes, tables of contents, introductions and publisher's blurbs. I stopped reading every book word by word, one page at a time from front to back, without looking ahead. That might work well for mystery stories, but it doesn't work well for theological texts. I gave up thinking I wasn't a good reader if I didn't read every book from beginning to end. Not every book is worth reading completely.

I began making better use of my limited time and energy for reading. I stopped wasting precious time trying to decipher sentences or paragraphs or whole arguments I simply didn't understand. Not every author is clear or reader-friendly. If the point was important, I could get help by talking it over with someone else. I stopped looking up the definition of every new word I came across. Some words were more important to the author's argument than others. I began listening for the author's key words, ideas, images and themes and learned to define them in context rather than just out of the dictionary. I stopped focusing on how difficult the text was and began focusing instead on what I understood. I didn't need to understand everything in a book. I learned to move back and forth between sections of a book the way I move back and forth in conversation with my friends. I began visualizing books as works of art rather than page after page of printed text. By reading less I began to understand more.

I also began facing reality. Reading theological texts isn't simply about understanding the great debates of past and present so I can join the conversation. It's an exercise in facing reality. Owning the truth about how I interact with books was just the beginning.

I forget when the light dawned fully. It happened sometime during graduate school. I remember the pain of waking up day after day realizing I had spent most of my life reading books written by men. Most were white men, but emotionally it didn't matter what color they were or where they came from. What mattered was that my reading life, like my life generally, had been ruled by men's voices. I grew up listening to men teach, lecture, preach, scold, correct, praise, humiliate, cajole, warn, shame and instruct me. Except for several women professors in college who taught nonbiblical and nontheological courses, I had never had a female professor. All my pastors had been men. Top administrators in my educational institutions of higher learning were men, except my college dean of women. In my Bible college only male colleagues had planned to go into ordained pastoral ministries. And though my seminary admitted women into theological education, the overwhelming majority of students had been men. Now it seemed the male authors of all the books I had read had come to life. They were joining all these other men in my life, a deep and confident chorus of male opinion and interpretation. The library stacks didn't feel as friendly as they had before.

It wasn't as though I'd never noticed this. In fact, I thought I'd coped fairly well. I had somehow agreed within myself that when it comes to theological texts, male gender usually doesn't matter that much. Since the author isn't physically present, his gender has somehow been neutralized. I didn't need to be concerned about this aspect of the author's point of view unless he was writing about obviously gender-related matters, such as the status of women in relation to men.

It hadn't occurred to me that gender affects points of view no matter what is being discussed. In the absence of clear gender bias against women, I believed I was on safe ground with male authors. I didn't need to take into account anything but the outer structure of the author's argument.

Now my age of innocence was over. I was furious at the system in general and horrified at my own collusion. The oft-repeated opinion that most theological texts had been written by men did little to appease me. I felt trapped. By my very participation in theological education I was lending credibility to a world of thought that had intentionally and unintentionally silenced the voices of women.

Over the years since, I've begun to discover the wealth of theological texts written by women. Discovering even small portions of this hidden body of literature is like discovering small portions of myself. I grieve over lost years of dialogue with women authors in theology. It isn't as though this literature just became available in the last decade. It was always there, waiting to be read. It had been easy to believe there just weren't many women who had written theological texts. This neatly absolved me from the extra work of seeking out these apparently precious few voices. Besides, I didn't want to get labeled as a female theologian whose only interest was women. I still needed to be accepted by male theologians.

In the short term I had a more pressing dilemma. Having come to this awareness, I didn't know what to do next. I was confused and overwhelmed. Of course I would continue reading women's theological texts. But how would I deal with countless male authors I'd spent years reading and trying to understand? I needed to reeducate myself, starting with reading overlooked books and articles. But I also needed to reexamine my inner dialogue with authors. For years it had been shaped and directed by men's agendas, men's questions and men's answers.

By this time I'd already begun preliminary work on my doctoral dissertation. I had decided to investigate Barth's doctrine of humanity, particularly his theology of male and female. I intended to demonstrate that Barth had actually argued for equal partnership between men and women and that other less favorable reviews were in error. I was going to rescue Barth for humanity. My encounter with Barth around this issue transformed my relationship to authors of theological texts, female as well as male.

It began when I discovered the importance of going beyond my first reading of theological texts. My initial reading of Barth surfaced more truth about me than about the text or its author. This reading was important. I learned about myself and my outlook on Barth. But I learned very little about Barth's point of view. Nor did I begin coming to terms with Barth's own words and meaning.

My second reading began the long, sometimes tedious process of discovering what Barth meant. I didn't want him to be clear about male priority over females. But he was crystal-clear. My initial reading had overlooked his clarity. My desire to protect him was an attempt to protect myself from the impact of his convoluted but ultimately clear description and justification of male superiority. It also protected me from the reality that these words had been written by a male theologian whom I greatly admired. Separating out the various strands of Barth's lengthy argument gave me a way to begin responding to him. But it did nothing to change his betrayal of female humanity or my despair that he had done this with the best of intentions.

Second readings can become surprising sources of grace. As I worked to understand the inner logic of Barth's many words, I began to notice repeated references and allusions to "the neighbor." I checked earlier and later volumes of his *Church Dogmatics*. Was I simply hearing what I wanted to hear? Slowly the image and theological importance of the neighbor emerged. Reflecting on Luke's parable of the good Samaritan, Barth discerned a truth about human relationships: Our humanity depends from the very beginning on having neighbors, people who see us in our need and help us gladly, no matter how small the deed. Without neighbors like this we won't survive. They appear when least expected and from the ranks of those with whom we would often rather not be seen. By their sometimes awkward or unwanted presence they remind us of our neediness. They also remind us that we're not alone in the world. In this passing and necessary ministry they are a sign that God hasn't forgotten us.

The distance was short between Barth's understanding of the neighbor and a new way of understanding how women, children and men are potential neighbors to each other. Jesus embodied the good news even as he proclaimed it; the good news isn't the priority of males but the priority of the neighbor. This isn't the neighbor for whom I do good deeds out of the supposed priority of my gender, age, rank, knowledge or riches. Rather, it's the unexpected, sometimes feared or hated neighbor who ministers to *my* need. Without such neighbors I won't make it in this world. These neighbors are also needy. But I won't recognize this unless we first meet on common human ground, not ground defined by my supposed advantage.

I began wondering whether Barth was my theological neighbor. Was there room for us to meet on common human ground? I couldn't change his mind or rescue him from his sometimes uneasy commitment to male priority. But in dialogue with him I had begun to discover other ways of thinking theologically about all human relationships, not just those between men and women. And I had begun to understand more clearly my own humanity and the ways of God with us. For this I was deeply grateful.

Other authors quickly began taking on flesh and blood. I felt as if I was coming out of a great fog. I realized I had never known how to think theologically about my relationship to authors as human beings. I didn't know how to join them in shared time and space. Their words were accessible on the printed page, but the authors themselves seemed to be out there in orbit beyond me. They were a strange company of disembodied experts who inhabited library stacks and bookstores. No wonder it had been easy to deny the significance of male authors' gender.

Seeing authors as potential neighbors means accepting not just my own humanity but theirs as well. It means accepting their natural human limitations and their fallenness. We stand on common human ground.

As a reader I'm constantly tempted to rewrite authors' books and lives in ways more pleasing to me—or to write them off completely. I'm put off by mind-numbing abstractions, misleading overstatement, unfortunate choices of words, inattention to important distinctions, and contentiousness. Sometimes I hear life described in ways that leave little or no room for my experience of life. The trouble in church and society is variously traced to all evangelicals, all feminists, all Westerners, all white racists, all heady academicians, all dour Calvinists or all overzealous Christians. The indexes and footnotes of most theological books record little attention to the many voices and concerns of women. Sometimes I hear undercurrents of violence or contempt, sometimes open rage. Scorn is heaped on movements and approaches to theology that have been life-giving for me. A religious journal reports the moral failure of yet another well-known author. There's more than enough not to like, not to agree with, not to approve of.

Every author is my potential neighbor, not a potential target. This is especially true of authors whose theological assumptions I don't share and authors I've avoided for any number of reasons.

I owe all authors the benefit of the doubt, whether I read them closely or merely skim their books and articles. I owe them the admission that in the end I may have misunderstood or misconstrued their arguments or their points of view. I owe them a special duty since most of the time they aren't physically present to speak for themselves. I owe them gratitude for having taken the risk of making public their thoughts and beliefs about theological matters. I owe them the truth about my current response to what they've written. And when they have unknowingly ministered grace to me in my need, I owe them gratitude no matter who they are or how they seem to perceive me or my world.

This approach to reading theological texts may seem naive and unrealistic, not academic or scholarly enough. I can only witness to my own experience. There are many reasons I read theological texts. I want to be connected to more points of view than I encounter in my church or my seminary teaching. I need to check out my impressions of particular authors or theological movements. I want to find out how fairly an author has been interpreted. I would like a better grasp of theological issues I encounter from day to day. I want to find out what other theologians are saying about issues that matter to me. I may need simply to refresh my memory.

But reading theological texts has always been about more than this. I've been on a search, listening for voices out there in the wilderness that resonate with my experience of life. I'm not looking for a mirror image of myself. I'm looking for anyone who knows where I've been, who has found in Christianity a source of strength and hope. I'm not looking for answers. I'm looking for food. Food for thought that is also food for my hungry soul.

In our process of becoming theologians, God invites us to begin relating to authors as potential neighbors. Like us, they seek to explore the meaning of God's creation, salvation and coming redemption. God invites us to listen not just to their ideas but for what compels, energizes and moves them forward. To read them from the inside out. To put ourselves in their shoes. To understand not simply what they say but why they say it and why it was important for them to commit these things to writing.

Reading theological texts in this way brings me closer to authors, though an irreducible gulf always remains at the end. It also brings me closer to the truth about myself, as the thoughts and meditations of my heart become visible in my inner dialogue with authors. Sometimes when I discover surprising connections with authors, it becomes a way to receive just a little of that food I didn't expect to find right here and now.

6

Theological
Etiquette

I LEARNED WORKS RIGHTEOUSNESS around our family dinner table. If I ate everything on my plate, I would get my reward—dessert.

Actually, it wasn't that simple. Many small works of righteousness were required. Come promptly when the dinner bell is rung. Wait to begin eating until everyone's plate has been served by your father. Don't complain about portions or gag on food you don't like. Don't wolf down your favorites. Don't talk with food in your mouth or chew with your mouth open. Don't make sucking noises as you drink. Don't overload your fork or push peas with your fingers. No elbows on the table. No playing with food on your plate. No playing with your silverware or fidgeting in your chair. No arguing with your sisters or talking back to your parents. And don't forget to say please and thank you.

Family meals weren't lessons in honesty or grace. They were occasions for practicing proper manners, eating whatever was put on my plate, learning to swallow things I didn't like (liver or okra) and figuring out ways to keep my feelings to myself without letting them spill over onto my face or into my body language.

When my sisters and I managed to do all these things well, there was plenty of good humor around the table. There was also plenty of bad humor: getting disgusting things down my throat (liver or okra) or being given more (liver or okra) so I could practice getting them down properly, or watching my younger sisters get the same treatment and being unable to intervene on their behalf. We relieved the tension by laughing at each other as we struggled to be obedient and avoid punishment. Most difficult of all was the discipline of hiding what was happening on the inside. Showing or telling the truth was out of order; it made things worse for everyone.

The need to be right in my father's eyes was ingrained in me at the family dinner table. If I did things right, I wouldn't get into trouble or make trouble for others. People would admire and look up to me as a child with superior training. I would be better than they, though it would never do to say so out loud. By my example I would show others this more noble way. My hosts and hostesses would reward me with attention, smiles and kindnesses not doled out to crude or rude children. My parents would be proud, and I would get my reward—dessert at the end of the meal, plus all those intangible extras reserved for proper young girls.

I needed to be right. My parents' reputation, indeed the reputation of our entire family, was at stake. My father's ability to control his household was put to the test every time the six of us sat down to eat. We most definitely were *not* like other families we thought we knew. These other families never sat down together at the same time. Children ate only what they wanted to eat; talking back and ill manners went unpunished; and everyone still got dessert at the end. Our family practiced good table manners. It was part of our Christian witness, a sign that all was in order in our family.

Etiquette is about how we relate to each other. Sadly, the

etiquette practiced around our family dinner table fostered isolation. I sat there next to my sisters and parents, agreeable and compliant most of the time. But emotionally and spiritually I was frequently a million miles away, isolated by fear of humiliation or punishment if my father decided I wasn't saying, doing, thinking or feeling the right thing.

For years the dynamics of our family dinner table haunted me in my theological work. I've sat down at hundreds of tables, often with authority figures to whom I assigned the same superhuman powers I assigned to my father. I brought with me a fierce need to be right, strengthened a thousandfold by my desire for white male approval. My Bible college, seminary and graduate training further reinforced the need to be right in matters relating to theology.

As a good girl from way back, I knew how to behave around the table. I wasn't pushy or arrogant. I remained silent unless absolutely necessary, speaking only after calculating and recalculating every tentative yet deeply felt contribution. When others reached out to me, I didn't know how to respond. Most of the time I felt isolated and lonely. I was deeply unsure of myself and sharply critical of others' theological ideas.

Theological etiquette is about relational commitment, not about getting the fine or even large points of doctrine all straightened out. It's about learning to sit down together face to face. Beginning to see and know each other. Beginning to listen and learn. Beginning actively to appreciate, honor and depend on others at the table. It's about learning to join with my table partners instead of checking them out to see how they're doing on the correctness scale. It means giving up patterns from childhood that keep me isolated in a supposedly safe and superior position—patterns such as separation from the world, ignorance about others, keeping all the rules, jockeying for position, speaking only when spoken to and not asking too many questions.

Theological etiquette isn't about skin-deep niceness and courtesy. It's about taking a deep breath and making space for truth to emerge. Not doctrinal truth in carefully crafted propositions, but relational truth that invites us to explore connections between what's happening right now and what we believe about God and God's world. It's about acknowledging concretely the presence of God's Holy Spirit among us. It's about accepting our human limitations and knowing we'll be attracted to self-serving points of view no matter how pure our intentions.

In my theological work, salvation means giving up attempts to justify my own beliefs and behaviors. It means allowing God to replace my anxious need to be right with an equally powerful need to understand others by making connections with them, even though I'm sometimes uncomfortable with them at the table.

My conversion didn't begin at seminary or in church. It began in support groups of women, men and young people of other faiths and no faith who came together out of common need. It began when I was lost as a Christian, needing to be found by God. I hadn't planned to sit down with these people around tables of any kind. I'm sure my parents hadn't envisioned this for their eldest daughter who always seemed mature and sure of herself.

Slowly, as I listened to the voices of my new table companions, I began hearing God's voice. I began to discern how isolating my works righteousness had been, how many walls had been erected by well-meaning individuals between me and other human beings. I began to glimpse how deeply I would need to go in order to begin again not just as wife, mother and daughter but as theologian, church member and faculty colleague. Nothing was out of bounds, including my theology. Not just the theology I write and speak about but the theology of my life. Not simply what I do but how I do it, so that I'm trusting God rather than my own rightness or my paralyzing fear of being wrong.

The rules of theological etiquette that work for me are deceptively simple. Actually they're not rules at all but exercises: spiritual exercises that engage heart, mind, body and soul together. These exercises take as much intention and practice as any other life-changing discipline. There are three of them.

The first exercise is to *speak truly.* Becoming a theologian isn't about learning when and where to say all the right things. It's about speaking truly. For me this always begins with giving up silence that supports my need to be right. By retreating into silence under the guise of listening, I was able throughout seminary and much of graduate school to maintain my own point of view without offering it for response and discussion. Sometimes silence was a way to survive a hostile or judgmental atmosphere. Sometimes I withheld myself from conversation because I thought there was nothing further I could contribute or learn. On the one hand, my thoughts and questions seemed trivial, irrelevant or naive, not worth mentioning in the presence of others who seemed more astute, articulate and sure of themselves. On the other hand, my mind was often already made up, so that further discussion didn't seem necessary or productive.

As a theologian, I need to open my mouth and hear my own voice at the table. I need to speak, whether I think my contributions are important or not. And as I speak, I must speak truly. I must put into words what has happened to *me,* what *I've* seen, heard and handled of life with God and God's creatures.

Speaking truly doesn't mean saying what I think someone else needs to hear. Most of my life I thought "speaking the truth in love" meant delivering unwelcome news—news about how some other person had offended me or the community by erring in thought, word, deed or belief. As the reluctant but determined bearer of this so-called truth, I didn't feel at all implicated in the offending matter. I was acting as God's spokesperson. I was there to deliver a message. The truth about the other person seemed perfectly clear. Now there was this nasty but necessary task to be carried out, the task of "speaking the truth in love." All for your own good, of course.

This isn't speaking truly. To speak truly is to bear witness from the place in which I presently stand. Theologians are human beings. I speak not just from within my God-given limitations but from within my fallen perceptions and responses. I do this always, though I may not recognize how it looks on me today. I can't assume the other person is the major candidate for change. I *can* assume that when I speak truly there will be changes in me. Speaking truly means bearing witness to *my* questions, assumptions, experiences, beliefs, observations, discoveries and struggles. Further, it means doing this without constantly looking over my shoulder to see how I'm doing.

I know I'm speaking truly when I'm willing to be caught in the act. Caught in the act of being human instead of appearing omnicompetent and all-knowing. Caught with my limited experience of life showing. Caught feeling defensive. Caught being rude to my table partners. Caught sounding certain of things about which I know little or nothing. Caught not knowing what to say next or how to respond to every question. Caught with my feelings showing in my voice or spilling all over my face. Caught in assumptions I thought I had left behind. Caught saying things that betray the secrets of my heart.

Being caught in the act isn't a disaster. It's an invitation to relax, to acknowledge God's gracious presence in the awkwardness, tension and confusion of the moment. Sometimes it's a golden opportunity to laugh at the absurdities of our common humanity. It may lead to self-examination and repentance. It may even be a huge load off my shoulders. It takes inhuman energy to script, choreograph, carry out and defend perfection.

The second exercise, *listening truly,* is the indispensable other side of speaking truly. Most of my life I didn't know there was a way of listening truly. I thought listening meant being pleasantly attentive, asking leading questions and letting the other person do most of the talking. But beneath this apparent receptivity my mind was usually racing. I listened for weak points in arguments or mistakes I was sure I would never make. Sometimes I interrupted the speaker out loud. More often I interrupted by talking to myself inside my head about why the speaker was wrong and I was right. Or I listened for places where I might indirectly turn the speaker to topics I thought more important or points I wanted to make but was afraid to voice. I took in and processed information, gleaning insights that might buttress my own point of view. I listened for ways I thought I might gain the speaker's approval or attention. I worked hard at appearing competent and knowledgeable, even when I felt lost.

What mattered in the end was what others thought and felt about me. Even when I worked to understand the speaker's perspective on the subject matter, I wasn't focused ultimately on what she or he might help me see. The bottom line was where I believed I stood in relation to the speaker. I needed to be right and to gain approval at the same time. I became adept at retaining a secret one-up position, even on the slimmest grounds. This required vigilance. If I let my guard down to attend fully to other people's experiences, beliefs and feelings, I might lose my edge of moral if not intellectual superiority. Worse, my point of view might be challenged.

Listening to men has been particularly challenging. As a theologian, I've been surrounded by highly verbal and vocal men, most of them white. I've been immersed in their theological worlds. Seeds of violence lie just beneath the surface of some of these worlds. Sometimes they spring up openly in words of contempt, ridicule or dismissal of other Christians or members of other faiths. More often they hide in methods that encourage theologians to separate ideas from their contexts, reason from emotions, the privilege of speaking as a theologian from the prior responsibility of listening, the work of theology from the work of self-examination. I don't want my theology to carry seeds of violence nurtured by retreat into abstractions, lonely isolation or the need to be right.

I used to think I could avoid this by becoming aware of it, speaking out against it and constructing a different theology. But it's too late. As I listen truly to the experiences, beliefs and feelings of all my partners around the table, I'm faced with my own collusion. I carry within myself patterns of thinking and living that allow violence to go unchallenged, especially violence around the table.

It isn't enough to begin recognizing ways my compliant female silence was justified theologically and enforced outwardly by both women and men. This is but the beginning of grief. When I listen truly, I also recognize ways my alien silence grew into a comfortable cover not simply for noninvolvement but for contempt. Contempt toward others and toward myself. Contempt that does violence in thought, word and deed. Contempt that silently scorns other voices and snuffs out compassion. As surely as violence has been done to me, I've passed it on in my work as a theologian.

Around theological tables we're all needy and vulnerable. There are no pure heroes or pure victims. Each of us stands between generations, struggling to live truly with what we've inherited and with growing knowledge of what we've already passed on and are still passing on. There's more than enough anguish to go around, and no room for self-righteous posturing. As we gather around work projects, mission opportunities, committee assignments, faculty meetings, worship services, special lectures, conference papers, classroom tables and church board meetings, we are living, breathing human beings. We don't need disembodied ideas and insights or opportunities to deliver more messages from God. We need to begin knowing each other as human beings.

We're needy and vulnerable. Yet we're needy and vulnerable in different ways. When we sit down together, I can't assume we're automatically on a level playing field or that what's comfortable for me is comfortable for you. Because I've been silenced, I must take the risk of talking out loud. For some of my table partners this seems a breathtakingly simple matter. For me it can be terrifying. I'm still getting used to the sound of my own voice. On the other hand, because I've tuned speakers out in my internal rush to protect and maintain my own point of view, I must also risk being silent. I must listen truly, as though hearing for the very first time. I must put aside understandable anxiety about not being heard or understood and give the speaker the gift I want for myself: the gift of a listening ear.

Speaking and listening truly isn't about being right. It's about taking risks with each other that move us closer to the truth about how God is with us. In those moments we aren't merely speaking or listening truly. We're living truly, living the truth about our need for each other and our reliance on God for the outcome of whatever happens between us as theologians. We're taking the risk of being caught in misunderstanding and the equally awful risk of being heard and understood as though for the very first time. We're meeting on common human ground, trusting God to direct us to a place where we can stand together, if only for a moment.

Speaking truly and listening truly couldn't be further from my early understanding of what theologians do. As a child, I thought becoming a theologian meant learning to debate. It was all about winning or losing. It was about marshaling the best arguments to support my position against yours. What counted most was logic of the head, control of data, recall of facts and the ability to poke holes in the other person's argument. It didn't seem important whether or how the issue being debated was connected to our lives or our relationships with one another. What mattered was demonstrating how right I was and how wrong you were.

Unfortunately, authority figures always seemed to win, and the debate never ended. It kept going in my head. Had I presented my best arguments, in the best order? Had I left something out or said something I regretted? Second-guessing was the order of the day after theological debate. Lying awake listening to reruns and feeling totally exposed to ridicule was the order of the night.

As I went through seminary and the doctoral program, I still focused on the need to be right. Becoming a theologian meant gearing up to do battle. Sometimes the model of warfare was appealed to explicitly and enthusiastically. At other times it was appropriated more subtly, under the table so to speak. According to the debate model, ideas would be the major casualties; nothing was supposed to be taken personally. In the warfare model, people themselves, individually and as groups, were the casualties. Every weapon was bent toward laying the enemy low in defeat, attacking wherever the enemy seemed weak. Character and style were as vulnerable as ideas and beliefs. Taking words or statements out of context was modeled, condoned, even encouraged. Twisting the truth in order to triumph was acceptable. The so-called enemy wasn't engaged with integrity, and usually wasn't even present.

Inwardly I relished the warfare model. Outwardly I became adept at a more benevolent way, the way of the physician. The analogy seemed right and laudable. Theologians diagnose what's wrong with other people's theologies, prescribe the needed medicine and administer or supervise treatment. There was no visible urge to win a debate or declare victory in battle, just the simple desire to help other people have the best theology possible. They hadn't studied these things extensively for themselves or couldn't think about them as clearly as I. In any case, they weren't aware of the many dangers and pitfalls that lie in wait for unsuspecting believers. My help was more than praiseworthy; it was essential. Someone needed to point out where other people were going wrong and what they needed to do to get back on track. I was more than willing to take charge.

The allure of these models is ever present. But this isn't where the work of theology is done. These ways of relating to each other steal time, energy and creativity. They bear bitter fruit as we become ever more calculating, manipulative, suspicious, defensive, isolated and lonely. They distance us from the possibility of speaking and listening truly to each other as human beings. They crowd out the fruit of God's Holy Spirit.

Speaking and listening truly are indispensable to the work of a theologian, but they aren't yet enough. Another exercise is needed. I must also *keep company with strangers.*

Early and often I was warned not to speak or listen to strangers. It was the main rule to follow whenever I left our house. Little girls or women of any age who got into trouble because they spoke or listened to strangers were simply reaping the consequences of their foolish behavior. The same rule applied in theological matters. Strangers were people who believed differently from the way we did. Of course you couldn't always tell who they were, since some of them looked just like our family. But most of the time they gave themselves away immediately by their dress, manner of life or family history. I grew up fearing strangers. I didn't want to get into trouble or lose my faith.

As a theologian, though, I must keep company with strangers. Giving them a smile or friendly greeting as I pass them on the street or in the hallway is a beginning, but it isn't enough. We must get around to speaking and listening. This means sitting down together, spending time together, learning to welcome each other at the table God has prepared for us.

It isn't difficult to identify strangers whose company I must learn to keep. They're all around me. People who don't know when to stop talking. People I wish would stop talking and listen to me for a change. People I've avoided because I don't know how to start a conversation with them. People with whom I'd rather not be seen spending time. People I think I already understand perfectly well. People I'm convinced agree entirely with me. People who don't seem to care whether I exist. People who consistently misunderstand and misrepresent me. People whose theology mystifies, irritates or alarms me. People who don't like theology because it creates more problems than it resolves. People I think don't belong at the table, and people who would be happier if I weren't there either.

Keeping company with strangers isn't about celebrating diversity around the table. It's about giving up my need to be right. It's possible to sit down at tables with theologians of every possible difference and not be inclined in the least to let go of our need to be right. In fact, this need may be intensified beyond belief precisely *because* there are so many differences around the table.

Keeping company with strangers means being committed to speaking and listening truly all the way around the table. It means being willing to make the first move, especially with those most strange to me. It means making room for others and not always sitting down at the same table or with the same agenda. It means seeking out the company of women, men, young people and children who don't think, talk or act like I do. It means honoring everyone at the table, knowing that I too am a stranger and the table doesn't belong to me.

Though I know all this in my head and have lived enough of it to know it works, I'm constantly tempted to assert my need to be right. Sometimes I feel an almost inescapable urge to move in and *do* something. I'm afraid that if I leave the battlefield the enemy will triumph. Falsehood will prevail. Centuries of injustice and violence will go unchecked—all because I didn't seize the opportunity to point out someone else's errors.

This is tricky. I was taught to doubt and give up my voice in deference to male voices and authoritative female voices. It's also tricky because giving up the need to be right isn't the same as accepting inappropriate speech or behavior toward myself or anyone else at the table. Giving up the need to be right doesn't mean giving in to whatever transpires. It means I'm free to say what's in my heart, not just about the topic of conversation but about what I think might be going on around the table, especially in me. I don't have power to change anyone else, much less to change the ever-present powers that work to keep us distant from each other. At the same time, my voice needs to be heard directly, not filtered a thousand times through my need to sound right, look right, act right and please all the right people.

I also need to remain open to further insight. I know I'm in trouble when my voice rises and I stop listening, especially to people who don't seem to agree with me. Sometimes I can't wait for the speaker to take a breath so I can jump into the discussion and argue for my point of view. I become so focused on points I want to make that I lose the opportunity to know and understand better my table partners—or to have my vision broadened by their perspectives not just on theology but on me.

Some might argue that this way of relating works fine when we're talking about work projects or plans for the future but not when we're talking about theology. If there's ever a time when we need to be right, it's when we're dealing with matters of doctrine. Truth is truth. There are nonnegotiable absolutes. This way of going about theological reflection seems to blur the truth. In fact, it sounds like anything goes.

Giving up the need to be right isn't the same as giving up my theological commitments. In fact, the more willing I am to gain further clarity about my rock-bottom convictions, the more willing I'll be to speak and listen truly and to keep company with

strangers. Not because I know my convictions are right, but
because I trust the power of God's truth to find and keep me no
matter where I am. Well-grounded theological commitments are
no guarantee that I won't lose my way. Nor do they release me
from the need to explore these commitments in the company of
strangers.

The need to be right in theological matters often masks fear
of falling into error. There's an element of truth in this. In genuine
conversation I take the risk of moving close to someone else—
close enough to hear and feel the truth in his or her perspective,
not just close enough to analyze ideas. When my theological
vision is enlarged by the life and perspective of someone who has
been a stranger to me, I may feel deep gratitude and humility. I
may also fear I'm making a big mistake, especially when this
enlarged vision means changing my comfortable routines and my
friends don't understand. Change isn't simple, including change
that helps clarify the meaning and implications of my most basic
theological commitments.

Theological etiquette isn't the stuff of big campaigns. There
isn't a grand finale when winners will be rewarded for their
diligence or all our theological visions declared pure. This is
about relational commitment over time. It happens in small
gatherings here and there, over many days and many conversations, in fits and starts. Sometimes we'll feel wonderful about our
progress; other times we'll be utterly lost and feel we're going
backwards. Indeed, we *will* need to back up often so we can begin
moving forward again. There's no grand prize at the end. No
dessert for good girls and boys. Instead there's the ever-present
possibility of being heard, understood, recognized or appreciated
as though for the very first time—not simply as theologians but
as human beings.

As for our theology, we and our theologies remain in God's
hands. Not in the hands of our table partners, and not in our own

hands. When we're ready for the truth of our humanity to show around the table, we can count on God's Holy Spirit to carry us through the ups and downs of genuine encounter—loosening our fearful tongues, calming our racing minds and hearts, opening our inner ears, giving us courage to look into the mirror and report what we see, guiding us together into paths of truth and right relations with each other.

7

Developing Theological Imagination

THE MOST GLORIOUS THEOLOGICAL INSIGHT I've ever had came to me as a child. The hymn line "Let every kindred, every tribe, on this terrestrial ball" evoked then as now an elegant, Cinderella-like ball. We were all dancing gracefully around the ballroom floor. Jesus himself greeted guests at the grand entrance. Heaven on earth would be a great, majestic, elegantly moving dance in honor of the Lord of all. Given the no-dancing rule in my house, this was a particularly colorful and joyous image.

Only after I'd begun teaching and was in my forties did I discover that the terrestrial ball was this planet earth. I was stunned by the extent of my commitment to the dance, not just by the seeming enormity of my childhood misunderstanding. To this day, whenever I sing this grand old hymn of praise I'm carried away to a great dance for all the peoples of this earth, hosted by Jesus Christ.

Theological imagination is about what things look like. It's about seeing into reality, discovering how the strange and ordinary pieces of our stories fit into the strange and extraordinary pieces of God's story. It's about taking another look. It's about listening for layers of truth in what's before our very eyes.

Picture this: It's a hot, humid day. I'm sitting on the edge of my waterbed. This means I'm sitting on the narrow edge of a plank of wood. I'm bending down to catch the light of a small lamp by the bed. The light from the lamp feels like a furnace. I'm straining to see the white part of my fingernails so I won't clip them too short. I've already butchered one. My seat is hurting, and I'm beginning to sweat. I feel irritable and edgy. I also feel like a martyr—gritting my teeth and bearing it in a bedroom that has bad lighting, bad seating and bad air.

I keep going. I know there's a well-lit, comfortable seat in the den just across the hall, with a lovely fan turned directly toward the sofa I could be sitting on. I could get up and go to the next room. I resist this easy and pleasant solution.

Several sweaty minutes later I decide with some effort, and not a little guilt, to put my bodily comfort first. I move to the den and resume my task.

As I work, I can't stop thinking about how difficult it was to give up doing my fingernails the hard way. It occurs to me that this love of doing things the hard way runs deep in me. I feel like a good girl when I do things the hard way. Others may take their ease; I, on the other hand, am committed to toughing it out. It gives me just a little edge of righteousness. Reason to feel just a bit superior. More praiseworthy. More likely to be singled out for honorable mention.

I don't like this revelation about myself. Given the choice, I'm likely to opt for doing without, to pass up a friendly offer of help or to stay home and study instead of going out to have fun with my family. It seems I'm hooked into thinking I'm a better person, even a better Christian, if I do things the hard way. Just look at all the daily sacrifices I make.

The connection to sacrifice brings to mind Jesus' death on the cross. Jesus died so I wouldn't need to sacrifice myself in order to be righteous. I already know this with my head. It pains me to confess I don't yet know this with my life. I think I'm earning extra credit for doing things the hard way. In fact, I'm far more likely to climb up on the cross all by myself than to allow someone else to nail me to it.

For whom am I doing this? Sometimes it feels as if I'm doing it for myself, to assuage some subterranean guilt about enjoying life too much. Sometimes it feels as if I'm doing it for the world, to help maintain a better moral balance in the universe. I want to position myself clearly on the side of all that's good, sober, responsible and worthy of praise, even though no one sees my good and joyless deeds but myself. With a jolt, I realize I'm bound by works righteousness. Getting up and moving into the den was one small step toward repentance.

Theological imagination is the heart of theological reflection. Without it theological reflection becomes repetitious, boringly correct and eventually blind to what's right in front of us. It becomes mere thinking *about* rather than seeing *into*.

My early training didn't encourage theological imagination. Facts were facts. God had already ordered all things and told us about it in the Bible. My role wasn't to wonder but to take good notes and give right answers. I was a diligent student. In my attic I have reams of paper given over to the recording of right and useful answers. They're full of wonderful truths about God and God's ways with us. They're also full of unexplored theological jargon.

Stock phrases and theological terms can be deadly to theological imagination, no matter how revered they may be. Some are as ancient as the church; others represent our best current efforts to clarify Christian identity. They roll off the tongue easily, eliciting nods and grunts of affirmation. But they stifle theological imagination when they occupy unexplored space in my mind, block doorways or keep at bay all signs of uneasiness or questioning. They seem to sum up whole worlds of meaning and truth. They become a kind of shorthand, assuring us that we believe the same thing or see things the same way even though we may be poles apart.

Development of theological imagination begins when I'm able to wonder about things I think I already understand, able to ask questions and turn things over in my mind, looking at what's in front of me from more than one angle. It's the end of taking things for granted. It *isn't* the end of truth about God and God's ways with us. Rather, it's the end of taking for granted my past and present understandings of that truth.

In Bible college most of what counted for theological work was research into biblical terms or biblical models, with connections made to the present by way of rather direct application. Seek after this; avoid that. Follow twelve strategies in church or mission work. Beware of six pitfalls. But one of my professors did things differently.

Mr. Hatch was unpredictable. His mind wandered and wondered and turned things over until we were sitting on the edges of our seats. Life, theology and the Bible came alive, not just once but every time we gathered for the next exciting installment. I couldn't get enough of it. It didn't occur to me that I might learn to do this for myself.

Years later, in seminary and graduate school, my theological imagination got set in motion. My professors didn't set out to teach me this directly, but they set the stage by requiring us to analyze pages and pages of theological writings and by showing us some of their own work. At first it was overwhelming. I couldn't imagine myself doing anything more than learning to summarize and explain other theologians' work. I immersed myself dutifully in reading assignments.

Along the way I began to get hooked, not so much by the

brilliance of well-argued passages as by the honesty of human beings searching for God and the truth about God's intentions toward them. I found theologians who connected with my heart, whose witness wasn't hidden beneath an endless stream of weighty words. As I looked into their biographies and the circumstances in which they found themselves, I began to know them better—not just the content of their writings but why they cared so deeply about what they had seen that they were willing to spend hours putting it into carefully chosen words. From time to time their written words ministered to me as profoundly as the spoken proclamation of the gospel. I was witnessing theological imagination at work.

How did they do it? At first it seemed almost magical. Some theologians just had a way with words, and others didn't. As I began working on the sometimes complex inner logic of theologians who spoke to my heart, I made a discovery: *less is more.* Where I had expected to find a dazzling array of impossible theological acrobatics and esoteric interpretive moves, I found instead simplicity. The key to theological imagination seemed to be a few thoughtfully chosen, reliable points of reference that fit each theologian personally. One size didn't fit all. It wasn't about having a bag full of tricky methods or being born already knowing how to make all the right moves.

My relief was enormous. There was hope for me as a theologian. I didn't have to attend to everything in the universe at once or try to make something out of nothing. I could quit my anxious search for suggestive metaphors and images. I didn't have to embark on freewheeling flights of fancy into esoteric systems of thought so that I could come up with something utterly unique. Nor was I confined to sitting passively under a tree hoping a theological insight might drop into my lap someday soon. All I needed were a few thoughtfully chosen points of reference that fit me, and the willingness to keep coming back to them. Not because there is anything magical about them, but because they mark the places where God has already found me and waits to meet me again.

It took a while to identify those places and how God meets me there. The first two seemed to come with the territory. I knew I could rely on the Bible and on the true witness of Jesus Christ. I couldn't imagine theological reflection without them. At first the other two seemed irrelevant and potentially dangerous: my own experience and strangers. I'd been taught to leave my own experience outside the door when I did theological reflection. Experience was untrustworthy. It would lead me to create God and the world in my own image. Suspicion about the value of human experience suited me fine, since I thought my life experience was pretty boring and trivial. I'd also been taught to do my theological work privately, not publicly. Of course there were certain trusted teachers and authors who would guide and shape my thinking. But keeping company with strangers wasn't part of the process. Strangers were outsiders to be converted, avoided or seen only indirectly, through my teachers' eyes.

Over the years I've come to rely in different ways on each of these four points of reference. But I didn't become clear about all four at the same time. Rather, I came through the door of my relationship to Jesus Christ.

I grew up knowing Jesus loves me. Jesus loved all the children. I didn't speak easily in public about my relationship to Jesus, but I knew I could count on Jesus. Some songs about him seemed too sentimental, but I enjoyed singing them along with everyone else. I didn't question whether Jesus was the Son of God. Of course he was. He was also a real human being who lived and died for me. My Savior. The Lord of my life. I was surrounded by church friends who spoke easily and often about their relationship with Jesus. It seemed there was this one relationship to Jesus that everyone was supposed to be developing. I felt self-conscious because my relationship didn't seem to fit the pattern.

In Bible college I began relying on the words and motion of music to give expression to my relationship to Jesus. I just couldn't seem to put it into my own words. I listened to friends speaking freely about how Jesus had met them that morning and what a wonderful friend he was. They felt close to Jesus and couldn't imagine going through the day without him at their side. I felt warmed and distanced at the same time. I was happy for my friends, especially those who had strayed away and then been found by Jesus. But I also felt distant and became increasingly ashamed of my lack of warmth for this man who loved me so much that he died for me.

In seminary I tried to put my discomfort away. There was work to be done, and though the question of my relationship to Jesus surfaced from time to time, it wasn't the main item on my agenda. I was surprised and comforted when I discovered that some of my new friends shared my uneasiness. We dealt with it by distancing ourselves from our past communities of faith. Their language and way of being with Jesus just wasn't our way. We decided we had left all that behind—not because we didn't care about Jesus Christ but because we were finding other things to focus on in relation to him. The intimately personal focus seemed less mature, less scholarly.

Following seminary graduation I returned for one last course, a seminar in the life and thought of Søren Kierkegaard. He was a stranger, a theologian unlike any I'd encountered thus far. For ten weeks we worked hard to keep company with him. His portrayal of Jesus Christ was astonishing. There Jesus stood in the Gospels, repeatedly calling out the invitation to come to him and rest. Most who passed by took one look and fled. They desperately needed rest, but the man issuing the invitation was ugly. Unattractive. Disturbing to behold. Was Jesus really like this? Was I running?

I began graduate studies and found yet more to wonder about. According to some theologians, unexamined language about personal relationship with Jesus Christ is a large problem in the church today. It's a crutch, a way of getting through hard times without taking initiative to change things. It drains away precious energy needed for the struggle against injustice. I was attracted to this perspective but uncomfortable because it was directed toward church members who looked like I did. Although I didn't know how to describe my personal relationship with Jesus Christ, I hadn't given it up. And I knew I wasn't a dropout from the struggle for a more just society.

Others raised even more difficult questions about Jesus. We say he's the Savior of the world and that in his work of salvation he experienced life as we experience it. But how could any man know what it's like to be a woman? And how could any man save women from situations in which men might be the villains? In fact, don't exhortations to sacrifice ourselves as Christians play right into the hands of men who exploit women? The questions were shocking. They touched some of my discomfort about my relationship to Jesus, but I didn't know how to name the discomfort, much less what to do with it.

I began dissertation research, determined to do my homework and complete my degree. I'd chosen Karl Barth as my dialogue partner. I knew Jesus Christ was the central figure in his theological reflection. I wanted to see how this worked for him, especially how it worked out in his reflection on relationships between women and men. I also knew Barth found in Jesus Christ support for the priority of men over women. I wanted to engage him in conversation around this issue. My relationships to men seemed to be at stake. I didn't have my relationship with Jesus Christ in mind as I began my research.

Barth's description of Jesus Christ reminded me of Kierkegaard's. Barth didn't use my familiar church language of personal relationship with Jesus. Instead he talked about encounter with Jesus. The Gospel witness to this encounter portrays it as both disturbing and full of promise. It's full of promise because Jesus Christ shows us the way back home to God, who created and redeems us. But it disturbs us because in Jesus we see not a strong man who towers above all others but one afflicted as we are in body and soul. Around Jesus is gathered a company of women, children and men likewise afflicted—hardly the cream of society. In him and in this strange company we see ourselves. Being close to Jesus is about finding myself in this company, not about rising above it.

This wasn't everything Barth said about Jesus Christ, but I knew this was about me. My discomfort intensified. I wanted to know more, and I knew I was on dangerous ground, not doctrinally but personally. Within the dynamics of my encounter with Jesus I would discover the truth about myself, not just the truth about Jesus. I would also discover the truth about God. In fact, Barth had already introduced me to the gracious God whose ways with us are revealed in Jesus' ways with us. I was ready to hear that God, like Luke's good Samaritan, looks on me with compassion and kindness. I began to find persuasive ways of talking about what it means to relate to Jesus as the truly good neighbor who reminds us that God hasn't left us alone in this world. I counted on the power of these insights to carry me through. Surely now I was close enough to Jesus.

Insights are moments of unspeakable grace, no matter when or where they come. Several years into dialogue with Barth I was standing in chapel singing "What a Friend We Have in Jesus." We came to "In his arms he'll take and shield thee." I felt as though a bolt of lightning was going through my gut. I couldn't get the words out of my mouth.

Why would I feel safe in the arms of Jesus? He wasn't just a neutral being. He was male. I didn't have a history of feeling safe in the arms of men. In fact, my experience had taught me to be wary and suspicious of men who wanted to get close to me.

The insight wasn't about Jesus' being unsafe. It was about the way I was relating to Jesus. My fear of genuine encounter with Jesus was connected to experiences with men who hadn't shielded me.

A huge and shameful burden began to roll away. There were reasons for my reticence to use the language of personal relationship with Jesus. The truth about my history with men was related to the truth about my history with Jesus.

I wasn't sure what to do next. I decided I didn't have to sing the words of any song about Jesus that stuck in my throat this way: not because Jesus wasn't my friend but because I wasn't sure how to relate to him in his masculinity. The intellectual coping strategies I'd used over the years began falling away. Though I didn't feel close to Jesus, the truth about the way I related both to him and to language about him was finally becoming visible. I wasn't just afflicted in my soul. I was afflicted in my body and my soul together.

For months I stood silently when phrases of songs and entire hymns triggered this emotional truth in me. Sometimes I wept. I wondered whether anything would ever change. At first I felt unspeakably lonely. But as I began talking to trusted friends about my experience, I discovered I wasn't alone. Not everyone understood, but some did. This wasn't just my private problem with Jesus. I wasn't dreaming, and it wasn't a small matter.

One day, in a seminar I was leading, the truth about my relationship to Jesus came spilling out. I'd been reflecting on it in the context of the seminar, trying to find a way to put it into words that didn't leave me stranded with nowhere to go. I'd had a germ of an insight, but I wasn't sure what to make of it. I didn't want to bring it to the group without letting them know where I was coming from. My heart pounded as I retold how I made the connection between not feeling safe in the arms of Jesus and being wary about getting close to men. Again some understood. This time they included men.

I tried giving words to my insight and found more words as we talked together. It seems each of us must negotiate a relationship with Jesus that fits who we are—men as well as women. Men don't have an edge just because they're men. Jesus is a stranger to men *and* to women. Further, he isn't a stranger to all of us together in a few predictable ways. Rather, he's a stranger in ways that become visible only when we risk moving closer to things about Jesus that we've ignored or tried to neutralize. According to the Gospels, Jesus isn't just another male. He's *this* male, with *this* calling from *this* God. He doesn't relate to human beings in general. Rather, he relates as *this* man to *these* women, children and men. And he relates in *these* ways.

Whatever my relationship to Jesus might come to look like, I realized it would be worked out slowly, one piece at a time. It would take on the shape of my salvation, and I would become a witness to how this happened. Not in neutral, generic language about salvation, but in words that told the truth about how God had found me.

I'm not suggesting there are a hundred different versions of Jesus for a hundred different people. The only Jesus I know is Jesus Christ as witnessed to in the Gospels. At the same time, just as I develop my own relationship to any one person you and I may know in common, so with Jesus. We can count on him to respond to each of us just as we are, according to the particular afflictions of soul and body we're ready and willing to have brought to gracious light. In the same way that I work out my relationship with the Bible, I work out my relationship with Jesus Christ.

I'm also not suggesting that salvation is a private affair just between Jesus and me. Coming to Jesus just as I am means becoming visible to others in my need, though not always at the time or place or in the ways I would choose. It means taking the risk of requesting prayer for myself, not just for others; accepting help instead of trying to figure out everything by myself; discovering in conversation with trusted friends how to begin breaking shame-filled silence about my life. Then, as I'm taking small beginner's steps, it means discovering unexpected connections between learning to trust Jesus and learning to trust my family and friends.

God has found me where I live and where I was dying—in my world, not someone else's. My experiences in life matter. God has found me in the Bible, especially in the Gospel witness to Jesus Christ, but also in passages where God seems absent or not very inviting. God has found me in the company of strangers: sometimes in their writings, more often in real life. And God has found me in Jesus Christ—not once but many times.

Theological imagination doesn't take these points of reference and turn them into a step-by-step procedure. The goal isn't to make something happen, but to go to these places and spend time there. Waiting. Wondering. Turning things over. Not everything all at once, not my entire life history or every thought and feeling, but whatever has my attention right now. Pieces of the Bible. Pieces of my relationship to Jesus Christ. Pieces of hymns, sermons and prayers. Movie themes and images I can't get out of my mind. Current events I'm tired of hearing about. Snatches of conversations. My response to the look on your face, or why I avoid sitting down at the same table with you.

At first I may hear nothing but silence. I may begin to doubt or explain away my own experiences. Maybe I misunderstood what was really going on. Perhaps I'm putting too much emphasis on the witness of the Gospels to Jesus Christ or relying too heavily on the Bible. I know many theologians who don't do it this way. And why should I pay attention to these strange and needy people who keep showing up in my life? What could they possibly offer me?

Though God has met me in these places and waits to meet me again, I still have fear and doubts. God met me last time. But maybe that was a happy accident.

When the silence becomes heavy, I often need to do a little troubleshooting. I go down the checklist of my four places, one by one. The fact that something is screaming for attention doesn't necessarily mean I'm listening. It's easy to find a hundred other things to think about, especially if what's really bothering me hits so close to home that I've turned down the volume. I know I'm back on track when I feel my adrenaline flowing.

Sometimes I need to face my fears, talking directly to them. Fear number one is that this way of going about theological reflection is too constricting. I might miss insights that other points of reference could open up for me. It's true. There's nothing magic about these four points of reference. Even when they're working, I won't discover every insight to be had about life with God and God's creatures.

It may seem that theological imagination is most free when it can range anywhere and everywhere. But for me this feels like looking through someone else's eyeglasses—blurry, disorienting and overwhelming. Everything may be in front of me, but it isn't focused enough to help me see what I need to see. Theological imagination isn't freed by removal of constraints. It's freed by acceptance of things as they are. Things as they are don't shut my imagination down. They open it up. They invite me to discover in what God has given me today, and in those places where God has found me already, more than enough to meet my need.

My greater fear is that the well just ran dry. I've used up my allotted insights for this life. From now on I'm doomed to hollow, predictable, deadening repetition of yesterday's discoveries. So I'd better pull out some of my old sermons and writings to see what I can salvage. Better yet, I'll borrow from someone else. This time the adrenaline rush isn't about getting too close to home. It's about being unmasked as an impostor. I'm just pretending to be a theologian. Everyone else already knows this. They've been wondering when I would finally catch on.

I remind myself that this is an old feeling. Furthermore, it contains a germ of truth. If I think theological reflection is about creating something from nothing, then I am indeed an impostor. God alone creates something from nothing. And if I think the only true witness for today will drop from my lips, I will surely be unmasked—not as an impostor but as the human being I am, needing to receive from others not just occasionally but regularly. Sometimes I *am* a dry well, waiting for rain from heaven, waiting on God and in need of a neighbor.

In this frame of mind I can turn to old sermons and writings, the Bible and other faithful witnesses—not so I can scrape together something that sounds respectable but to bring to remembrance the many ways God has found me in the company of sisters and brothers.

8

Speaking
in My
Own Voice

I COULDN'T FORGET THE LOOK on my mother's face when I opened my Christmas present from my grandfather. I was about twelve years old. My mother's father lived in California; we now lived in Georgia. Gifts and letters had replaced lively visits to his apartment. He was generous, funny and unbearably proud of his four granddaughters. We were the apple of his eye, the cream of the crop, the smartest and the best. He decorated his long typed letters with dancing stick figures and messages congratulating each of us on our latest accomplishments and adventures. In his eyes we could do no wrong.

That Christmas he sent us flannel pajamas. Not the same version in various sizes and colors, but a different style for each of us. I'd never seen flannel pajamas as feminine as the pair he'd chosen for me. They didn't have the usual straight-hem button-front top and elastic waistband bottoms. Instead the top was a short, graceful gown with a small ruffle repeated at the neck, on the long sleeves and around the long shirttail hem. The same ruffle decorated the bottom of each leg, which reached about midcalf. Powder-blue flowers were scattered across the warm white background. Every time I put them on I felt elegant and grown-up, like the young woman I was becoming.

But I couldn't forget the look on my mother's face when I took them out of the box. I determined in my heart to buy a pair for her. The noisy steam radiators in the drafty mid-nineteenth-century house we occupied rent-free weren't very efficient. I wanted my mother to be as cozy at night as I was, and to love the way she looked and felt when she passed by a mirror. I began a secret search every time we went to a department store. But these were California pajamas, not for sale in Savannah, Georgia.

Right after Christmas I wrote the usual thank-you note to my grandfather. My parents had strict rules about thank-you notes, especially to him. More than once I'd rewritten notes that hadn't passed inspection. We weren't to mention amounts of money he'd sent but what we had purchased with the money. Though we were overjoyed to receive cash, we weren't to tell him so or hint in any way that we'd needed or hoped for cash. If he sent expensive gifts, we weren't to be too effusive about them. It was important not to sound fixated on money, on the cash value of things or on him as the source of unusually grand gifts.

Now I needed my grandfather's help. I tried to find out casually from my mother how much the pajamas might have cost. I counted the money I'd saved up over the weeks, including a little I'd gotten for Christmas. I needed at least two more dollars. My father owed me allowance money at twenty-five cents a week. Without explaining why I wanted it, I requested what was owed and offered to do extra work around the house to earn the rest. When he questioned me, I said it was for a good cause; he would understand later. He said he was sorry, but he couldn't give me the money right now. He didn't have it, and even if I worked to earn more he wouldn't be able to pay me. I waited several days and asked again. He still didn't have the money. He seemed upset, especially since I wouldn't tell him why I wanted it. I felt awkward and guilty for putting him on the spot.

I decided not to wait. I wrote my grandfather a letter. I said I wanted to surprise my mother with a pair of pajamas just like the pair he'd sent me for Christmas, but I couldn't find them in Savannah. I told him her size and asked him please to buy a pair for her and send them in the mail. It was January, and she needed them as soon as possible. I sent the money I had and told him I would send the rest when he let me know exactly how much they cost.

He replied immediately. He was thrilled to be part of the plan. The pajamas were in the mail and the bill had been paid in full. I was overjoyed.

When the package finally arrived, my scheme was quickly uncovered. My mother loved her new pajamas with their powder-pink flowers. She was also caught off guard by my initiative. Perhaps she didn't want her father to think she wasn't being properly taken care of. My own father seemed torn between gratitude and distress. I'd broken the rules about what I could say in letters to my grandfather. But how could he punish generosity? I was glad the complicated negotiations were finally over and I hadn't gotten into trouble.

This is my first memory of speaking in my own voice. Sadly, it was a major exception to the rule. Most of my life I've been afraid to talk about my plans or dreams, afraid to take initiative about things that matter to me, afraid of putting my thoughts and feelings into words. My family and the churches I attended as a child and teenager were more interested in outward conformity than in encouraging me to find my own voice. I survived by retreating behind strategic silence and strategic speech.

Becoming a theologian is about giving up this kind of silence and speech. It's about letting others in on what I'm thinking about and how I'm responding to what I see, hear or read. It's about not being afraid to speak with my own voice. It's about accepting God's invitation to be myself, not someone else real or imagined.

Just be yourself. Most of my life I believed that being myself was precisely the incorrect, inappropriate and unacceptable thing to do. My self was foolish, inept and only marginally attractive. I had to pretty myself up, especially if I had a part to speak. I needed to make sure my hair was combed, my slip wasn't showing and my dress was modestly neutral in color and style. I spelled out every word I would say, writing them down and rehearsing in advance, making sure I'd covered every angle. I didn't want to be accused of overlooking a crucial point and thus be discredited. I worked hard to say things in just the right tone of voice. I didn't want my carefully prepared words to be dismissed because my attitude was judged unacceptable.

Learning to speak in my own voice has been and still is the most challenging part of becoming a theologian. It has taken decades. Ever since childhood my female voice has been shamed, overlooked, disbelieved, punished and silenced more times than I care to admit. There haven't been many women around to show me the way.

For years I denied I'd been hindered or affected by any of this. When my voice didn't seem to be getting through, it was easier to blame myself. I didn't want the same things to happen to me that were happening to other women I knew. I believed I would be heard as a theologian if I worked diligently and avoided the mistakes they were supposedly making.

This is nonsense. Preparing my lines and modulating my voice ever so carefully doesn't guarantee I'll be heard. I will never turn in a performance so nuanced that no one could possibly dismiss or misunderstand me. I know because I've tried, and I lost my voice in the process—not once but many times.

Giving up attempts to control how people might respond frees me to get on with the work of developing my own theological voice. This means attending not just to actual speaking events but to what goes on before and after, internally as well as externally. The work is intensely personal and painfully public. My students, colleagues, friends and family live through some of the work and some of the pain with me. What do I want to say? How will I say it? Do I want to say all this out loud and in public? Will I be able to respond to questions and comments? And what's going to happen when I get home? Will I be able to sleep at night? How will I take care of myself if I begin falling into old patterns of replaying lines in slow motion, second-guessing myself?

It takes time and energy to decide what to say and how to say it. Then it takes more energy to say it. The most important part seems to be getting the words out of my mouth. Once that's done, I'd like to be finished and have everyone agree with me. But speaking as a theologian is a relational act. It isn't a one-woman show. Nor is it simply the communication of information and directives or my best arguments for a point of view. It's an attempt at making connections and a confession that I need your listening ears and your responses. It's an opportunity to speak, think and act together on things that matter to all of us.

When I arrived at seminary I didn't know what I wanted to say as a theologian. I just knew I'd needed to speak for a very long time. I wasn't sure how to proceed. I depended heavily on my professors and other theologians to suggest ways of talking about God, sin and salvation, or what it means to be human. It felt safer that way. My words would make more sense if they echoed what someone else was already saying. Besides, I was happy to support and advance their good work.

My early goal was to avoid danger. I didn't want to sound as if I was about to go over the edge, especially when I began talking about male-female relationships. I defined terms carefully and surrounded each slightly innovative thought with a thousand qualifications. I didn't want to lose my faith or my credibility. I worked hard to demonstrate that my theological ideas were well grounded.

As time went on, my theological agenda began to take shape around gender relationships. I began by responding to approaches that seemed oblivious to women or assumed women are junior partners to men. I clarified what didn't make sense and what I didn't want to perpetuate. Usually I started with how women had been left out of the picture and then pointed out where the theologian or document in question had gotten off track. Sometimes I developed my own insights, but my voice focused on pointing out what was lacking in other theologians. I believed this was the most positive service I could render for women. Surely my reasonable and well-researched approach would be persuasive.

I wanted to help end the madness, especially against women. But theologically justified rules and regulations still support repression and violence. Theologians caught in tragic human circumstances still pass on a legacy of suspicion and joylessness. Churches and families still pay dearly for a pastor's or parent's theological blundering and blindness. More to the point, speaking out against these evils didn't guarantee that I hadn't already fallen into them. Furthermore, though I wanted my theological work to benefit women, I didn't have a positive theological agenda. I could point out problems and list reasons we needed to change our ways. But I hadn't discovered persuasive ways of pointing to something better or describing how we might begin moving in a different direction.

When I left seminary and began graduate school, I still hadn't found my theological voice. So far most of my work had been in written form, for my professors. The few published pieces I'd written about women were coauthored with my husband. I was terrified at the prospect of taking responsibility for my own voice not just as a graduate student but someday as a professor.

By the time I began research for my dissertation I knew what I wanted to do. Women had been overlooked for centuries, especially in theology. Instead of spending most of my time pointing out this great omission, I would begin making room for all women, children and men. Virtually anyone would be able to find themselves somewhere on my theological map. It would be a good place. No denigration and no invisibility.

I became energized. How did other theologians bring women's thinking and experience of life into theological reflection? How would I do this, given my theological commitments? What language could I find to communicate a persuasive, inviting vision of God's ways with us and our ways with each other?

In the last chapters of my dissertation I tried out my new, inclusive voice and suggested an agenda for further theological reflection. My professors congratulated me on a job well done and signed the title page of my dissertation. Surely the next step would be development of insights into the dynamics and theological significance of human relationships, building on what I'd just completed.

Was I speaking in my own voice? My words bore witness to what I understood of God and life up to that time. They rang true to my deepest longings about relationship with God and with people God had brought into my life. My mind and heart were being changed by the good news about God's gracious ways with us. God's grace freely and joyfully surrounds and supports our relationships with each other. We need God and we need the people God brings into our lives. Most wonderful of all, I wasn't put here to figure out everything by myself or to die a thousand lonely deaths inside. Being broken and needy isn't proof of a disobedient, proud and rebellious spirit. It's a cry for help.

By the time I finished my dissertation I'd been teaching three years. Opportunities for speaking in public came regularly. So did terror—not about what I wanted to say but about the actual event of speaking. I usually got through on the outside. But I wasn't making it on the inside. I had a clear message, and most of the time it seemed to be well received. Yet from year to year I felt myself shutting down inside instead of becoming more relaxed and confident in my role as professor. I could sit at the piano and play all the right notes with a measure of ease and grace in my fingers, but my spirit was bound.

Something wasn't working. I felt trapped and alone. I entertained thoughts of an early retirement so I could give up public speaking and spend my time writing. This was pure fantasy, since writing was quickly becoming as difficult as speaking. I needed help.

For months a battle raged within. From one side, the battle was about whether things were really that bad. Down times are to be expected. I would get over it. Besides, who promised teaching would be easy? What made me think I shouldn't have problems? Everyone has problems. Things aren't that bad. This too will pass. From another side, voices from my past sternly reminded me that every problem is ultimately spiritual. I was wasting my time trying to figure out if things were really that bad. I needed to get down on my knees and repent of my sin. It was time to resubmit myself to God's will and ask God's forgiveness for my obviously proud and rebellious spirit. Then there was my body, also raging within, screaming for attention and finally propelling me beyond this futile and destructive inner conflict. I picked up the phone and asked for help.

This call for help marked the beginning of intentional work on discovering and developing my adult speaking voice. It was a first step toward breaking the silence that had bound me since childhood. In spite of my early determination to succeed as a woman theologian, it had become easy to think of myself as one of many powerless women who weren't being heard or appreciated. Women's not being heard and appreciated *is* a large problem—but my problem was still larger. I didn't know how to listen to myself, much less how to appreciate what I heard.

For the first time in my life I began keeping a journal and talking to a professional counselor. Instead of dismissing my past as water over the dam or as typical family history hardly worth talking about, I began looking into it and describing what I found. Instead of taking family patterns of communication for granted, I began wondering why things were the way they were. With help I began to see the larger family system, the role I'd been assigned to play and how very well I'd learned my part.

I saw that my childhood retreat into strategic silence and strategic speaking may have spared me some pain then, but it was paralyzing me now. Unfinished family business was intruding into my professional life. My voice was shutting down. I didn't know how to maintain clear boundaries around my time and energy. I said yes when I wanted to say no, and no when I wanted to say yes. I panicked inside every time I dealt with deans, presidents or board members. I didn't do much better with colleagues or students. Sometimes I felt competent and clear. But often I was one scared little girl inside, intimidated by a glance or a look on someone's face, tongue-tied and terrified that I wouldn't pass inspection. That it didn't show on the outside was beside the point. It showed to me and it showed at home, especially to my husband.

When I was a teenager, my piano teacher wanted nothing more than to free my spirit. Most of the time I got the notes right, with breadth of expression. But there was no passion in my playing. One day, clearly distressed over my inability to put myself into my playing, she asked whether I had a lover.

I was shocked. How could anyone ask a good girl like me about something like that? I was also embarrassed. Reluctantly I admitted the truth: I didn't have a boyfriend. She sighed ever so slightly and told me I needed a lover.

Mrs. Hanks was right. I needed to fall in love. Eventually I did, followed no doubt by the desired results in my piano playing. Now as an adult, many years later, I needed to fall in love again, this time with truth. Not just with knowing the truth about myself but with speaking it. Saying it out loud, not just to God but to other people.

I began with a few trusted friends, including my husband. I told my children I was doing some homework and began talking with them about ways my family history had affected me as a parent. I started talking with sisters I'd not spoken with for years. Accompanied by my husband and my sister Diane, I made a long journey home to begin talking with my parents. Piece by painful piece I broke my silence of many years. I recalled events and patterns in our family history, things we'd never talked about with each other. I told them how some of this affected me back then and was affecting me now. I began expressing feelings I'd kept hidden away behind a thick wall of silence—negative feelings I'd never understood and wished would go away, positive feelings I'd wanted to express for years but couldn't.

Learning to speak with family members meant learning to listen actively instead of passively. I discovered I could engage in conversational give-and-take. For example, I didn't have to sit at my parents' dinner table feeling trapped because my father seemed to be doing all the talking while the rest of us did all the listening. I could actually suggest a topic for conversation and be part of it from the beginning. Or I could change the subject. At other times, in difficult conversation about the past or the present, I didn't have to shut down inside in order to survive. I could remain fully present, noticing what was going on in me and gaining clarity about other family members' perspectives. Considering their points of view didn't negate my own or my need to express it. If someone fell silent, I could ask that person about it later instead of presuming I knew what it meant. Listening helped me find ways of openly joining family members instead of withholding myself from them in lonely, awkward, silent isolation.

As long as I was bound by patterns of silence within my family, my theological voice was also bound. Not because I had nothing to say but because I'd become increasingly isolated within constricted, fearful patterns of speech, thought and life.

Giving up strategic silence and strategic speaking didn't solve everything overnight within my family or in my work with seminary students and professional colleagues. In some ways life has become more difficult and painful for all of us. When I speak in my own voice about troubling topics, I can count on tensions, unanticipated complications, misunderstandings, confusion, anxiety and distress, not just in my conversation partners but in me. I can also count on opportunities to consider other points of view and the possibility that with God's help we may find a better way.

Speaking in my own voice as a theologian means bringing my whole self into the room, not just words about God. It means giving no less and no more than I'm prepared and able to give today. It means speaking passionately, resisting the temptation to guard my speech and writing because the emotional truth might show. It's about involvement, investment in the subject matter. It's the opposite of cynicism about life, theology, seminary or the church. It's about staying in touch with reality because there's something at stake here for us and for our children. It's about opening my mouth to say what I keep waiting for someone else to say.

We aren't playing games or going through motions at home, in seminary or at church. What happens within these walls is inextricably connected to what happens beyond them. I'm passionate about finding connections. I thrive in places where connections are being made. Places where women, children, young people and men are letting go of their tentativeness. Places where we're learning to speak about ourselves and God with us, instead of talking about everyone else. Places where we're giving up fear of sounding naive or too accepting of others, fear of standing out in a group, fear of letting others see who we are and where God is finding us. Places where heart-to-heart words, tears and laughter aren't suppressed lest we appear too enthusiastic or unduly committed to learning, to ministry, to God and to each other.

Speaking in my own voice also means preparing myself before I walk into a room. Passion doesn't replace preparation. Having a good heart, a good text and a burning desire to speak doesn't mean I'm ready to open my mouth. Speaking about God doesn't automatically trump speaking about the weather. I can't presume God will transform my good intentions into useful insights. People aren't obligated to listen to me with more respect or attentiveness just because I'm a theologian.

I can't control how people respond when I speak. Nonetheless, I'm responsible for the words I use. I'm responsible for making sure they're mine from the inside out. Other people's words help me find my way, but ultimately I must take the risk of putting my own words out there—not packaged in someone else's manner of speaking but clothed in my own. I'm responsible for offering words that ring true both to the subject matter and to me as the speaker. Words as clear as I can make them for today. Words that leave room for me to come back tomorrow, should God grant me that opportunity.

I used to be afraid I would run out of things to say, use up my small bag of theological insights. If I had something to say today, I was that much less likely to have anything for tomorrow. I also thought theological insights dropped randomly from heaven to earth. If I discovered one it was a happy accident, not a sign that there were more than enough to go around. And so I had a second fear: fear that someone would beat me to it. Some other theologian would find "my" theological insight before I did and say everything before I could say anything.

It hadn't occurred to me that other theologians' discoveries might confirm and enrich my own. Furthermore, the intersection of our thinking didn't mean that we'd lived the same lives or that either of us could speak for the other.

It's easier to insist on speaking for myself than to give up my desire to speak for others. I used to fear that if I didn't speak for everyone, the limitations of my understanding would show. I would be guilty of overlooking the experiences of other people, just as other theologians had overlooked my experience. I thought inclusiveness meant being beyond reproach in these matters, or at least apologizing for the many points of view I couldn't represent. But as a theologian I can witness only to what I've been given by God and to what I've experienced of life. I can't speak for anyone else. Not for women in general, white women, my parents, my three sisters, my two children, my husband, seminary colleagues, evangelicals, Presbyterians or preachers' kids. I can't develop a theological position so inclusive that anyone will be able to hear his or her voice in what I say.

Every time I speak in my own voice, my limitations become visible, not just in my experiences of life but also in my theology. For every place I've been there are a thousand places I haven't been and never will be. For every point I make other considerations could be raised. I don't need to be defensive or apologetic. I can speak only in my own voice. At the same time, I haven't given up on inclusiveness. In fact, being inclusive is the best way to make sure I won't run out of things to say.

Inclusiveness isn't about getting the details of my theology just right so that everyone's concerns and points of view are represented. Nor is it about trying to understand other people better so I can pretend to speak for them and also for myself. It isn't even about being sure my language is properly inclusive. Rather, it's about how and where I relate to others. If speaking as a theologian is a relational act, so is being inclusive. The question isn't whether I give evidence of having considered you and your concerns in my theology but whether I'm willing to include you in my life. As part of my theological work, am I widening the circle of my life to include people, places and conversations I've been avoiding? Some limitations of my theology are invitations to widen the circle. Theology follows experience of life. If I run away from this lifework, I will surely run out of things to say.

9

Persevering

I'M ABOUT EIGHT YEARS OLD. I'm sitting at the dinner table, just around the corner from my father. The table is set, the food is spread before us, and we're all in our seats waiting to begin. We haven't yet asked the blessing. I'm playing with my dinner fork, just to the left of my plate. I've moved it a few inches away from my plate.

My father's voice interrupts me. "Elouise, put the fork back where it belongs."

I move it to the right, in the direction of my plate. "Elouise, put the fork back where it belongs."

I move it slightly closer. My father's voice remains firm and controlled. "Elouise, put the fork back where it belongs."

By now my sisters are watching to see what will become of me. My mother is silent. This has become an event. Slowly I raise my hand to my fork and move it ever so slightly closer to my plate.

My father persists. So do I. Many repetitions later he's satisfied; the fork has been returned to its proper place. He proceeds with the blessing. He doesn't know what I know: the fork is ever so slightly to the left of its proper place.

My father's mission as a parent was to train us to keep the rules. My mission as his child was to break and keep the rules simultaneously. Back then perseverance meant getting through another day, using whatever survival skills lay close at hand. If my father was persistent, I would be more persistent. If outward rebellions were too costly, I would invent creatively invisible yet superbly effective inward rebellions. If I was ordered to sit down and stop talking, I could continue standing and talking on the inside for as long as it took to comfort myself. Indeed, this was the better way. In the private spaces of my mind no one could put me down, refuse to listen to me or try to break my will. In a family system intent on turning out obedient daughters, I survived by being secretly disobedient.

Back then the rules wanted to do everything for me, whether I understood them or not. In fact, it seemed more virtuous if I didn't understand them. Blind obedience promised that I could be good without getting dirty. All I had to do was repeat after someone else. I wouldn't need to learn things the hard way. I could get there without experiencing life firsthand.

Of course I did experience life firsthand. But it was an isolated version of life, bound up in layer upon layer of rules large and small, spoken and unspoken.

Becoming a theologian has meant getting and staying in touch with life, especially when things begin heating up. This often means breaking rules openly, publicly, unashamedly and deliberately—not to make a point about breaking rules but to turn on end the rules that keep me locked into my own small world. It means going against intuitions and habits that for decades helped me be a good girl on the outside. It means changing behaviors and attitudes that keep me from people and places where God waits for me to join the work already in progress. God's work will proceed no matter how long it takes me to get there. But it won't be the same for me or for my companions if I'm not along for the adventure.

Perseverance is about surviving what happened yesterday and what's happening right now. It's also about thriving and getting ready for tomorrow. It means attending to little things now so I'll be ready for the big things later. It's about gaining inner strength for life to come, not just hanging on for dear life now.

Most of the time I work on little things. Daily chores and disciplines like getting out of bed in time to prepare myself for the day. Focusing consciously on God's presence and care. Breathing deeply when my mind and emotions begin reliving yesterday or racing ahead into tomorrow. Taking time to reflect and write a few paragraphs. Preparing and eating breakfast. Reviewing what I plan to eat the rest of the day. Packing lunch and filling a water bottle to take to the seminary. Not rushing as I get ready to leave the house and drive to work, especially when I'm later than I'd like to be. Staying home when I'm sick. Noticing what's going on in my body as I teach classes, sit in meetings and talk with students or colleagues. Stopping for lunch in the middle of the day. Closing my office door to take a break. Leaving for home in time to eat dinner and spend time with my husband. Getting to bed early enough to get seven or eight hours of sleep. Taking time during the week for physical exercise and for conversation with trusted friends and family members. Taking time at the end of the week to reflect on my teaching.

This has become the routine shape of my weekday life as a seminary professor. When these little things are in order I know I'm at rest, even when I'm in the middle of a storm.

Little things are more than habits of life. They're theological disciplines. They're one way I confess to God and to myself what I say I believe: I'm a human being created, found and kept by God. I'm not a robot or a well-oiled cog in an educational machine. I'm not superwoman, and I can't make it by myself.

Attending to the little things helps me make peace with my body as a good gift from God. My parents ordered our family life according to a potentially healthy routine. Even when there wasn't much food in the house, we sat down around the table, gave thanks and ate what my mother had artfully prepared and presented. We went to bed and got up at regular times. We received daily instruction about basic nutrition and routine health care. Chew your food well before you swallow it; brush your teeth at least twice a day; always wash behind your ears. I learned many right moves that serve me well today. Sadly, I didn't learn to befriend my female body. Absolutely necessary information about menstruation was communicated not a moment too soon. We didn't have safe, reassuring, open discussions about sexuality, or about aging and dying.

Back then my body seemed more like an appendage or tool than an integral part of my being. Unless I was physically ill, my body was to be seen (not too much, of course), not listened to. Emotions of anger, fear, sadness, dislike and frustration were routinely subdued or denied. So were feelings of great joy, delight, affection and desire. To its credit, my body was useful. With it I could work hard, anticipate and meet the needs of others, accomplish tasks and carry out assignments, perform for others, and work hard to make sure I did better the next time around. Today when I skip the little things, it's usually because I'm working hard to please someone else or to subdue my fear of not being prepared. Or my fear of enjoying life too much.

I learned to listen to my body the hard way. It began Friday of Holy Week, several years ago. I walked down the lane near my house and up the next block to the United Methodist church. It was noon, time for our neighborhood's ecumenical Good Friday service.

The small sanctuary was already well filled. I nodded to friends as I took my seat on a side aisle, about halfway toward the front.

Within minutes my body was in agony. I took several deep breaths, hoping the intestinal cramps and waves of nausea would go away. I sat through more of the service than my body wanted to sit through before I finally stood up and walked out.

When I got home the pain subsided. But it returned Saturday evening as I prepared for Easter Sunday morning. I knew this pain. It had been coming and going for well over a year, especially when I went to church or sat in chapel at the seminary. I had also been unpredictably and regularly overtaken by weeping as I participated in church and chapel worship.

My doctor had examined me, observed my intestines in turmoil and heard my despair. She'd made several recommendations about managing my physical condition and suggested I also begin work with a therapist. I'd begun that work two months before the Good Friday service.

Now the pain was more insistent than ever, and my mind was in as much turmoil as my body. The link between this pain and being in church was indisputable. It also seemed totally irrational. I'd been a faithful churchgoer since infancy. My parents had lifelong commitments to church work, and I'd been right beside them doing my eldest-daughter part ever since I could remember. I couldn't imagine missing Easter Sunday worship for anything other than a certified, recognizable physical illness or family emergency. But every time I even thought about going to Easter worship, my gut began screaming with pain.

I decided to listen to my body. I stayed home from church. I took care of my body and kept track of my responses to breaking the Sunday church rule. I stayed home a second Sunday. And within a few weeks I knew what I had to do. It was time to work on my troubled relationship not just with my family but with the church. In fact, the two relationships were so intertwined I scarcely knew where one left off and the other began.

I had never felt at home in church. Though I enjoyed seeing

my friends and taking part in church activities, I didn't feel I belonged.

When I was growing up, my parents always seemed to be searching for the right church. From time to time my father took on a long interim pastorate or a formal teaching assignment in a local church. I was always relieved when that happened. As long as my father had preaching or teaching duties every Sunday, I knew how to talk about what he did and where we went to church. I also knew we were in the right church. We were always warmly welcomed and urged to stay longer. In these good and open spaces people admired our family. They thanked us regularly and tangibly for the gifts each of us offered to the community.

But there were costs. I gladly accompanied my family on Sundays and participated in the programs of these churches. But I never sank deep roots in any one congregation. No matter how much I liked the people we were with, I was always aware that we were different. We were the pastor's family. As the eldest daughter I was sometimes given responsibilities before I was ready for them. Sadly, I don't remember having a pastor of my own or being an integral part of a congregation. I ached for close friends like other young people seemed to have, but felt distant from my friends at church. We seemed to lead only vaguely similar lives. Others knew when they were at home and when they were at church. I was never quite sure where I was. It seemed I was always in both places at the same time. Obedience to God and obedience to my parents, especially my father, were indistinguishable.

I joined the church on the outside. I learned to stand up in front of people and speak in public. I learned to keep going and keep smiling. I learned to be in church without being present to myself or to people next to me in the pew. I didn't pay much attention to what was happening on the inside. It seemed irrelevant. It also seemed to work well, especially when I began accepting leadership and speaking roles in churches as an adult.

I entered seminary. Almost overnight I was grateful to come each Sunday morning and just be part of a congregation. I was glad to be in churches that understood my academic workload and didn't pressure me to get involved. But I felt guilty. Though I was studying to be a church theologian, my participation in church life seemed to be shrinking.

Then I entered graduate school. It took every ounce of strength to make progress in my graduate program and attend to life at home with my husband and with two children entering their teens. I remained involved part time in music ministry and taught an occasional adult class. But I still felt guilty.

I began teaching in seminary while I was writing my dissertation. Once again I was relieved to find a church that understood my academic workload. It was wonderful to walk into church on Sunday knowing I wasn't expected to be up front delivering a lecture or facilitating class discussion. But I still felt guilty. I observed my male colleagues at the seminary. Every weekend most of them preached or taught in churches. I knew I wouldn't survive if I did that. But I wasn't sure how to talk about it without making apologies for myself as a theologian. In faculty meetings, colleagues regularly emphasized how important it was for seminary professors to be involved in local church ministry. I agreed. I regularly reminded my students that they couldn't be theologians without being active participants in their local congregations. From time to time I told myself I really needed to get this part of my life in better order.

Now my body was telling me the same thing. It was time to join the church from the inside out. For one full year I didn't attend Sunday worship services. During the year I stayed in touch with my pastor. It was difficult for both of us. Staying away from Sunday services felt forbidden and dangerous. Twice I attended services, only to have my body remind me why I had chosen to stay home. I began wondering how long this strange sabbath rest would continue. I became fearful lest students and colleagues at the seminary discover my Sunday absences. I didn't yet have words or understanding that would do justice to what I was going through.

That year I joined the church for the first time in my life. I began receiving pastoral care not just for acceptably packaged requests but for deep and heavy burdens I'd been carrying for decades. I began connecting with individual members of our church body who understood what I was going through. They sat with me as I wept and wondered where this was going and when it would end. With my pastoral therapist I began untangling childhood church and family matters from adult church and family matters. I found my voice and began speaking clearly with my pastor as his colleague in ministry and a church member under his care. I discovered the wonder of joining the body of Christ instead of remaining a perpetually different and disconnected spectator. I began learning to love and live with the church in the flesh instead of relentlessly reminding myself and others of its many shortcomings. I began taking my place alongside my sisters and brothers instead of avoiding them or needing to be in charge. When I returned to church on Easter Sunday one year later, my body and my spirit rejoiced together.

Meanwhile, work on church and family matters had already spilled over into my work as a seminary professor. This work was about public speaking, and it felt like another storm.

When I began teaching, I knew I would have public speaking opportunities. Indeed, this would be part of my work for the seminary. Though I'm not a very public person, I felt competent to take this on. I'd been speaking in churches for years. There would be challenges, of course, but they would be manageable.

During my first decade of teaching I accepted speaking engagements regularly. Not as many as my male colleagues, but enough to begin developing my public voice as a theologian. I was dismayed as preparation for these events became increasingly more difficult. I decided this was due to the subject matter and the increasing size of some of my audiences. I pressed on, grateful for each opportunity to add another entry to my résumé.

Now, in the middle of my one-year absence from Sunday church services, I was almost totally distracted by psychic noise. I was busy on the outside with classes and other seminary work, but my mind and emotional energy were driven by upcoming speaking events. Chronic anxiety troubled me. What would I say six months from now? When would I find time to work on it? What if I couldn't find anything to say? What if my presentation didn't measure up to expectations? What if I totally missed the mark and made a fool of myself? Why had I agreed to do this in the first place? My anxieties were so loud I couldn't hear myself thinking.

I decided to decline all extra speaking engagements for the year following my next major speaking event. I also decided to begin accepting new engagements only after that year was over. I continued to teach classes and carry out seminary responsibilities. But for a full year I didn't even consider accepting invitations to speak or preach. I wanted to know what it would be like to live without this psychic noise reverberating in me day and night. I wanted to reexamine this part of my life as a theologian and find a public voice more congruent with my inner voice.

It felt like a giant leap back. I was sure people would forget me, take me off their lists, decide they really didn't want to hear from me after all. I would definitely lose ground professionally. Worse, I might be labeled a bad girl who wasn't cooperating with the program. I might be thought not willing to do my share of public relations work for the seminary. Not willing to do my part for women in ministry. Not interested in furthering the cause of theological education. Not willing or able to carry out my calling.

During that year I did go backward. I began finding my public voice in the place I'd least wanted to find it: at home, in conversations with members of my family. Some conversations were like rain falling on parched ground. Others were like falling into a deep pit. I began speaking from my heart. Reluctantly, I gave up my lifelong habit of watching myself out of the corner of my eye. I stopped trying to phrase things so that no one could possibly disagree with me. Word by word, I learned to speak just as I was—not as I thought I ought to be, and not as I thought others wanted me to be. I began paying attention to others' responses and mine, instead of rushing ahead to the next thing I wanted to say. It was like learning to dance. Practice, practice, practice. Three steps backward, one step forward.

When I returned to public speaking at the end of the year, I felt relaxed on the platform for the first time in my life. Not because I knew audiences would accept or applaud everything I said but because my external voice reflected more faithfully my internal voice. I didn't have to cloak my speech in protective maneuvers. I could speak directly and clearly, without apology and without exposing every private thought and feeling. I could relax on the outside because I was coming to rest on the inside. My internal voice wasn't as likely to drive me to distraction with endless commentary on whatever I'd said in public that week. It was relinquishing its role as full-time monitor of whether I should or shouldn't have said this or that out loud. It was beginning to sound more like an ally, less like my worst critic.

All this and more has been part of becoming a theologian. Sometimes I long for the good old days. I want a set of rules that will carry me through unscathed and deposit me safely on the other shore. Sometimes I feel like giving up. Even taking care of the little things becomes overwhelming. And no matter how often I practice my other new survival skills, I'm not totally comfortable. I don't always like the way they feel on the inside or the way they might appear on the outside.

I'm anxious each time I ask colleagues or students for feedback, and I don't like receiving feedback when I haven't requested it. It feels like giving up my voice or handing over my reputation to others who will now speak inerrant and unwelcome truth about me. I don't like telling colleagues what's going on in my classes when I'm embarrassed, ashamed, puzzled or clueless about it. Surely by now I should be able to resolve things on my own. I'm uneasy admitting how deeply some events disturb me, especially events in the past. Everything seems fine now, so why bring it up and disturb things even more? My tongue feels like a lead weight when I talk out loud about difficult subjects. It's easier to shut down or look the other way. I don't like reading my own body language. I'm much better trying to figure out everyone else's. Gathering information doesn't come naturally either. I'd rather wade right in with my first-impression opinions. It's difficult to admit that some situations aren't safe for me and to insist on having a fully informed ally present. I don't want to seem uncooperative or untrusting. It's equally difficult to get up and leave when I find myself in a punishing situation. I might lose the little advantage I thought I had going into it.

I remind myself I'm not doing this simply for my own benefit. My personal discomfort isn't the point. In fact, discomfort with doing business the old way may be my best connection to tomorrow and to what matters for all of us. The old, familiar feeling that nothing will ever change is a luxury I can no longer afford. There's too much at stake for my children and their children, for my students and their parishioners.

I also remind myself I'm not doing this alone. In my seminary work I'm surrounded by colleagues, students and friends whose wisdom, courage and insight continue to amaze and instruct me. In my family I'm held by bonds of growing love and affection, even in the midst of heartbreaking family trials and tribulations. In my church I'm borne along by clouds of witnesses past and present, friends who understand what it means to be a beginner. I didn't get here by myself. I'm part of a great company.

Sooner or later I'll find myself again in deep water, caught in another storm. Maybe I'll see it coming and maybe I won't. It may be totally improper, inexcusable, unfair, unjust or unwarranted. It may be more or less predictable, especially in hindsight. In any case, I'll be pushed to live at the edges of my theology, without much time for reflection. I'll find myself in places where my witness of yesterday will be tried by fire.

I know this because it has already happened. Friends and family members I've counted on will leave. Some will die sooner, not later. News about a family member's health and well-being will again change our relationship overnight. Discoveries about my family's history will open yet another unexamined chapter in our life together. Someone will set in motion other plans for my life without consulting me. Individuals listening to me will project onto me the voices and attitudes of other women, especially women they fear. Others will hear me truly and be courageous enough to tell me what they hear. Friends and strangers will discuss me behind my back. Sometimes they'll agree on what's wrong with me and seek remedies without speaking to me directly. My body will turn another expected or unexpected corner, closing forever some chapters in my life and opening others.

Several years ago I was in my car, on my way to the first day of spring semester classes. I felt shaky and uncertain. A year earlier, students had lodged serious complaints against me. They were reported to me anonymously at the end of the semester: several pages, single-spaced and typed. I was devastated. The seminary president requested a meeting with my dean and me. I asked one of my teaching colleagues to accompany me. The meeting was long and difficult. I couldn't believe this was happening to me. My request to meet with concerned students was denied. Now, just one year later, several students who might have been part of that group were in the required course I was on my way to meet for the first time.

I stopped at a traffic light and waited for it to change. Two older men, perhaps in their seventies, were coming down the sidewalk, facing me. They were out for an early-morning walk. They moved along quickly, talking and laughing. The sun was up. It was a gorgeous day.

As they came closer, I noticed they were holding hands. This seemed rather unusual. But it was also wonderful. My mind turned to friendships among older men. I wondered how long these men had known each other and whether they walked together every day.

Suddenly, without any signal and without breaking their stride, they left the sidewalk and began walking through a large parking lot. They seemed to be of one will. As they angled away from the sidewalk, I saw it for the first time—the short leather strap they were holding between them. One of them was blind.

In a flash my eyes filled with tears. I saw myself walking blindly into this class. Seeing some things, but not everything. Knowing someone with sight beyond my sight was beside me. All I had to do was follow God's lead, keep holding on to the strap and keep putting one foot in front of the other.

It looked easy when I watched those two men. Almost effortless. But God knows, as they knew, how difficult it sometimes is to keep moving and keep trusting.

CPSIA information can be obtained
at www.ICGtesting.com
Printed in the USA
FSHW011953090120
65944FS

9 780830 815197